NE

George. T. Cooper.

First published in 1963
as ORDEAL IN THE SUN
by Robert Hale Limited

NEVER FORGET, *NOR FORGIVE*

GEORGE COOPER

NAVIGATOR BOOKS

Published by Navigator Books
Ringwood, Hampshire

ISBN 0 902830 53 8

Typeset by Moorhouse Typesetters
Printed by The Cromwell Press, Melksham, Wiltshire

CONTENTS

ILLUSTRATIONS

George Cooper. A photograph taken shortly before the war

1

"White Clouds of Summer"

"Abandon Ship."

The order came at the end of a grim fortnight aboard H.M.S. *Exeter* in the Java Sea.

As part of an Allied force we had steamed north from Batavia to intercept the Japanese invasion of Sumatra, but by the morning of February 15th, 1942, their troops had landed and their covering force was withdrawing northwards.

We were bombed all day near the Gaspar Strait, west of Borneo, but the ship was so well handled by the Captain (Captain O.L. Gordon, M.V.O., R.N.) that we were never hit. Later we were able to return to Batavia under cover of darkness.

We escorted a convoy of merchant ships, which had escaped from Singapore before it fell, through the Sunda Strait and well out into the Indian Ocean before dispersing them to their destinations. Then we turned and came back. I was walking the quarter-deck with the Commander, and as we entered the Java Sea I said, "There's the door slamming behind us."

"Yes," he said, "and we're on the wrong side."

Heavy enemy forces were closing in and the attack on Java was imminent. Against us was the whole might of the Japanese Navy, and we had only half a dozen cruisers of different types from four navies.

On February 24th, *Exeter* and the Australian cruiser *Perth* were moved east to join the Dutch forces at Soerabaya, and three days later we were engaged with the Japanese heavy units covering their assault on the north coast of Java.

During the course of this action *Exeter* was hit in the boiler room severing one of the main steam pipes to the engines, speed being reduced to fifteen knots. As the action was being fought at twenty-eight knots, we fell out and made our way to Soerabaya to make good our repairs.

Next day, we buried the fourteen men killed in the action, and sailed at dusk for Colombo. For some unaccountable reason it was considered at headquarters that our best means of escape lay through the Sunda Strait to the westward, whereas the chances of doing this successfully were very remote in such enclosed waters. It would have seemed wiser to get away to the eastward towards Australia, as a chase in this direction would have drawn the enemy away from his fuelling bases, which he could not easily afford.

The following morning, Sunday, March 1st, 1942, at 7.30, we sighted the topmasts of two Japanese heavy cruisers and turned south until they were out of sight, when we resumed our westward course.

At 9.30, we sighted them again to starboard with a large destroyer, and shortly afterwards two smaller cruisers with five destroyers appeared on the port side. We turned to the eastward with our escorting destroyers, the British *Encounter* and the American *Pope*, to put the enemy astern.

For two hours we had a running fight with them. They straddled us many times but never hit us until at 11.30 one shell penetrated the boiler room. It was a shot in a million as it cut our one remaining main steam pipe.

The ship just came to a stop in all departments. The main engines stopped through lack of steam. The dynamos stopped. The turrets were motionless on different bearings. The steering failed. The inside became full of smoke as escaping oil fuel in the forward boiler room burst into flames. There was nothing we could do except sink her.

So the magazine valves were opened. The condenser inlets were allowed to flood the engine room, and watertight doors usually kept closed were opened. A pretty good inferno was going on down below as the fire spread. She started to list slightly to port, pouring black smoke out of her funnels. I thought she looked defiant, like a stag at bay. Men were cutting down carley floats and flotanets, casting timber adrift, turning out boats.

The Japanese were starting to hit us now as the range closed in. The after superstructure caught fire and the whine of projectiles sounded like the *Ride of the Valkyries*. She was getting lower in the water and heeling more. The inside had been completely evacuated; no one could live down there. At the bottom of the ladder leading to the upper deck were a lot of people, all quite calm. She was very nearly stopped, and men were leaving in dribs and drabs. As they went they drifted away astern. Then I climbed over the side and jumped into the water.

A little later, a destroyer closing on the starboard beam fired a torpedo. It was a good shot as it hit her right amidships. The old dear shuddered a bit. She seemed to shake herself from bow to stern. She must have had very little positive buoyancy left as she went right over to starboard until her funnels and masts were horizontal. Then, heaving herself up in a final act of defiance, she disappeared in a swirl of water, smoke and steam.

I had never seen a ship sink in day time before. I had seen twelve ships sunk in a convoy in the Atlantic one wild night in October 1940. One of these I saw break in half and the two halves rear up in the air and disappear in twenty seconds. But darkness had spared me the most terrible sight for any sailor - a ship's final lurch below the waves when the ocean floods inside and gets her down forever.

So I shall never forgot the sight of *Exeter* going. It did not seem real. We had lived in that ship for a year. We had our cabins and messdecks there, all our private belongings and treasures, mementos of home, books, photographs. I remember throwing my own large Barr and Stroud binoculars on the deck before I went over the side. What a waste, I thought, yet a bagatelle compared to the loss of a fine 8-inch cruiser with a score that included the *Graf Spee* off the River Plate. Anyhow, we all gave her three cheers as she went. You could hear the faint cheers rippling over the water.

The wind was fresh and the sea choppy. The smallest lop is annoying when you are swimming involuntarily, and this was spreading the men out. Rafts drifted away from groups in the water swimming or holding on to anything that floated. Soon we were spread out over a wide area. A number of men were swimming aimlessly. Some would leave one group and swim to another as they heard or saw their chums. Friendship ties are very strong on occasions like this. We could see the Japanese cruisers disappearing over the horizon to the eastward. They were not waiting and we did not expect them to, when there was still unfinished business with *Encounter* and *Pope* fleeing in that direction. Besides, our submarines were known to be operating in these waters.

Then two destroyers suddenly turned towards us, one large and one medium sized. The large one had a big "3" on her funnel, and it struck me as being odd that the figure was not in Japanese. As they came up past us they sounded off the alert on their bugles. They had all their men fallen in opposite their action quarters, and as they passed, they stood to attention and saluted. We were amazed. We did not understand it at first, having rather expected a hail of bullets as we gathered that the Japanese did not believe in taking prisoners-of-war. These people seemed to be behaving differently from our expectations. It was a nice touch. A ship had been lost in battle, she had gone down fighting and all due respects must be paid.

They then just went in among the survivors and stopped. As they drifted down wind, they drifted on to the groups of swimmers who clutched at the lines over the side and were hauled inboard. Having got one lot, they would move over to another. I remember wondering whether it was worthwhile getting into their hands, but there did not seem to be any likelihood of anything else coming along and the idea of swimming forever in shark infested waters was not exactly stimulating. It was either being picked up by them or letting the air out of the lifebelt.

The big destroyer drifted past us twice but we were too far off to warrant leaving the flotanet we were hanging on to. Some men had left and tried to swim to her but it was further than they thought, as it always is, and she was past and drifting quicker than they could swim. I advised everyone to remain until the situation looked more favourable.

Eventually she moved upwind and came past again, this time fortunately quite near us. It was this or nothing and we took it. We had been about two and a half hours in the water by then, and it was quite enough. My legs were getting tired. I had been floating on my back with my feet out of the water and did not realise that the sun was burning them until they suddenly became most uncomfortable. The rest of my body was immersed or fairly well acclimatised to the tropical sun, and my head was protected by my anti-flash helmet which I still had on.

It was all I could do to get on a rope ladder, the bottom rung of which was on the water's edge. I remember noticing how light she was and how short of fuel she must have been; the barnacles on her hull were above the water line and hurt my feet.

Having got on the ladder, I could barely climb it. Nor for that matter could many others. However, exerting all my strength, I eventually managed it and arrived on the deck to look into a number of slit-eyed, ugly, expressionless faces. I had never seen a Japanese in his own element before, and it was not a very pleasant first impression.

A petty officer came up, took off my lifebelt and threw it on a heap. They did not have lifebelts in their ships then; they considered them unnecessary as they went into battle to fight to the death. If defeated they preferred to die. Later on, when they started losing all their trained men, they learnt the wisdom of trying to save a crew to fight again another day.

The P.O. said, "Knife-u."

I always carried a knife and had it in my pocket. He took that, which was reasonable, I thought.

"Offeezer or sailor?"

I said, "Officer," so was sent forward on the forecastle while the men went aft on the quarter-deck. I thought this was very good organisation. I am certain we had no one who could have said any of this in Japanese if the position had been reversed. They had removed dangerous weapons and separated the officers and men. All very right and proper.

On the forecastle I found about a dozen officers. We all sat down in a heap just forward of the turret, and were chatting away on a number of disconnected subjects. Then we became very silent. We had had a strenuous time since February 24th when we had left Batavia suddenly and gone to Soerabaya; after which we had gone out again to ward off the assault on Java, and sailed into the first battle on the 27th. Ever since dusk on the 28th we had been at action stations. We were mentally and physically exhausted and too numbed to appreciate the full implications of our defeat and capture. At the time nothing really mattered. Even in the water it had all seemed wonderfully peaceful after the crash of battle, and I had not seriously cared whether I was rescued or not.

Then they stopped picking up men. We saw a raft drifting past, but the destroyer suddenly went ahead and away. We saw the other destroyer doing the same, though hundreds of men were still in the water. We tried to point this out to the Japanese but they took no notice; they were just leaving them. We could see men waving in the water or on rafts, but could not tell whether as a farewell or in an effort to attract attention. It was terrible seeing our shipmates left there to drown. Soon they were far astern and out of sight, but as there was nothing we could do about it we soon ceased to worry. We felt flattened and quite apathetic.

We could see the Captain standing in the front of the bridge. He was tall for a Japanese and wore a white jockey cap. From time to time he smoked a cigarette, and every now and then gave an order to the officer of the watch. Otherwise, he was quite impassive; his face revealed nothing. He had just been through a battle in which his side had been victorious, yet there was not a glimmer of the triumph or pride he may have felt, not a sign of relief or fatigue. He never looked at us.

I think they expected more of our ships in the area as they were very alert. Their lookouts kept a ceaseless watch with great big binoculars on stands. The Captain was constantly scanning the horizon. It must have been an anxious time for him, all on his own in enemy waters and with little fuel. The course was north-east and the speed about fifteen knots. She was obviously going to fuel in South Borneo.

The Dutch admiral at Soerabaya had advised us to leave on Sunday night, instead of Saturday night, as he said they would be refuelling then. How right he was. We might have got away if his advice had been taken, but we had had our orders from higher authority.

The Japanese behaved very well. They never touched us, nor did they take anything from us other than our knives and lifebelts. After a while they counted us and gave us some biscuits and water. We expected to be very thirsty after swallowing so much salt water, but we were not so till the next day, when it was very bad. Actually it was the thought of being without water that really worried me that first day - I have a horror of thirst.

A Japanese sick berth attendant went round with a bottle of spirit removing oil fuel from people's bodies and putting on bandages where there were wounds or cuts. Their whole conduct was really exemplary, but not as efficient as it might have been.

This was the time to interrogate their prisoners - when we were still shocked and not quite in command of our mental and emotional resources. But to give them their due, they already had enough on their plate, apart from having to cope with about two hundred and fifty of us aboard, and about a hundred on the smaller destroyer. I think they left half of the *Exeter*'s company behind in the water only because any more would have meant risking capture of the ship by their own prisoners - there were only a few sentries with rifles guarding us; they obviously could not spare many men for this job in a battle area.

There was something wrong with their "A" turret. Men were coming and going, and they had stripped what looked like the pusher hoist.

By five that evening we felt more rested and composed. I remember warning everybody about the possibility of being interrogated and that we must be very careful not to give away any information. We then chatted for hours in low tones about the battle and what had happened. As we only knew the story in bits, it was interesting to hear about what had happened to others in different parts of the ship.

About nine - my waterproof watch was still going - there was an alarm and everyone went to action stations. They had sighted something. This was rather perturbing for us because we did not know what they would do with us if they went into battle. A little later we sighted a ship quite near and stopped. It was obviously one of their own, as they fell out their men and manned a whaler. The boat was lowered and sent over to the other ship, a merchant ship. A lot of signalling went on and eventually the boat returned and was hoisted. The two ships then parted and proceeded on their respective courses.

It got very cold in the night. They gave us a large canvas tarpaulin to cover us all, and we slept fitfully in two rows, feet to feet, huddled together. But the deck was so hard you could not lie in one position for long. Whenever you turned over, everyone else woke as the tarpaulin moved. The night seemed interminable.

When dawn came, we all stood up and stretched our stiff limbs. They did not like us standing up normally but they made no objection this time as it was obvious why we were doing it. The guard brought us a bucket of hot sweet milk and some biscuits. As he left he threw down two packets of cigarettes, and then produced a brass ash-tray with a slow match in it. That cigarette was like an elixir.

We seemed to be steaming up a wide river as we could see land on both sides and the water was discoloured. This was obviously South Borneo. In fact it was Bandjermasin. A little later we could see ships at anchor in the distance, and in half an hour we were close enough to distinguish them. Two big 8-inch cruisers with sloping funnels and raking bows of the Asigara class were coming out, one a flagship. These were obviously the two we had engaged in both battles, the ships that had sunk us. They looked very fine in the morning light moving out to sea.

There were several tankers anchored with destroyers fuelling. We went alongside a very large tanker of about 10,000 tons. We were interested to see how well the Captain handled his ship but were not impressed. It was softly, softly catchee monkey, as he crept up and stopped some way off. The seamen threw heaving lines very well, whirling them round their heads first like lassoes, and then warping themselves alongside.

As soon as the destroyer made fast, we were all moved off on to the far well-deck of the tanker, and herded there in a very confined space. These tanker Japanese were not very pleasant; they pushed people around and generally were rather arrogant. It was already extremely hot, there being no wind, and as the sun beat down the iron deck became unbearable to men unshod as we were.

You never saw such a motley crowd - some in rags, some in shorts only, some in overalls, some in just a sweat vest, nearly all of which were stained with oil fuel. No one had shaved for two days, and all were hatless except for a Royal Marine officer who still had his side cap and was as spruce as ever.

There were some badly wounded men too. Stoker Darley was in a terrible state, the whole of his face having been burnt by escaping steam. The salt water must have been agony. The skin came off in strips if you touched it. Someone had treated him with grease in the destroyer and put a handkerchief over his face. Now the whole lot had stuck together in a congealed mess. There was just a little space for his mouth. He was moaning and crying for water.

After some difficult conversation with the tanker officers, we got them to allow us to put the wounded in the tunnel running from the fore well-deck through the bridge structure, to keep them out of the sun. But we had to have water. These men would die, especially Darley, if we did not get some. All of us were suffering acutely from thirst. Already we had learnt the Japanese for water - *mezu*. We went and asked for some, but all they said was "*Nai*" or something like it; obviously it meant "No".

Later, one of them brought some water in a bucket and we gave it to the sick and wounded first. Darley was greatly relieved and was quiet and comatose for some time. Then we gave everyone a mouthful or two all round. The sailors managed to get hold of some more, and we had enough to carry us through the day without much discomfort. None of us was very hungry.

Darley was bad about midday. I thought he was dying, so I approached one of the Japanese officers, who spoke a little English, and asked if the destroyer's doctor could come over. He said he would ask, and later on the doctor came but did nothing. I think he did not know exactly what to do and considered it better to do nothing. I was quite certain Darley would die during the night. It was hot and airless in the tunnel and he was lying on the steel deck.

The Japanese rigged an awning over the well-deck to give some shelter from the sun and everyone clustered under it. Up to now life in this tanker had been really grim and our spirits were very low. We were being beaten by the sun, thirst and fatigue. However the little drink of water and the awning saved us, and we sat down to await the future, although it did not appear very bright. We were at least five or six miles from land which looked hot and unfriendly. Escape was out of the question.

About 2 p.m. a Japanese officer from the destroyer came over and said in quite good English that he wanted the senior executive officer and the airman. That meant me, and the Observer, P. Brougham. I did not like this very much though it did not surprise me. We went back on board the destroyer.

An officer took me down to the Captain's cabin which was under the bridge structure. It was very small, just a bunk and a table at which two could sit and nothing else, and facing me, sitting at the other side of the table, was the Captain. He motioned me to be seated opposite him, which put me with my back to the door which was about two feet behind me. I did not relish this position as I saw that at a signal from him to a man in the doorway I could get a sudden knife in the back or a cosh on the head. We had all heard grisly stories of Japanese savagery. So I managed to shift myself round to where I could see the door reflected in the scuttle glass.

The Captain had closely-cropped hair as is the custom with all fighting men of Japan, and I felt his steely slit eyes boring into me with unwavering penetration. In front of him he had some papers, signals and notes covered with Japanese characters, and a packet of cigarettes was standing up in the middle of the table. His face was like an expressionless mask, without sign of thought or emotion, as he silently studied my face. I found it difficult to return that look, so I looked away, all round his cabin, as nonchalantly as I could manage.

This went on so long that I began to get bored with the whole proceedings. He then started in very bad English, obviously learnt for the purpose in hand.

"You are my preesoner. I command you. You must tell me." He paused and I said nothing, so he repeated it, hissing the "s" in "prisoner". I nodded and he continued: "Where are the Amerikana soljars in Java?"

"I don't know."

"You must know. You must tell me."

"I don't know anything about American soldiers in Java. I am a sailor."

"You are my preesoner. I command you. You must tell me."

"We do not have military dispositions in ships."

"You are a senior offeezer. You must read military orders."

"I am only the third officer in my ship and I do not see secret orders."

"It is seekaret, eh? You have seekaret orders. You must tell me."

"I do not see secret orders in my ship."

"You must tell me. You no speak. I take you on deck. Fire, fire! You down, down!"

He patted his hand over his heart significantly and I thought I had better get him off the subject of secret orders. Actually, I knew nothing of the military dispositions in Java and had never heard of any Americans being there yet, though the wireless had mentioned that some were being sent.

"You must tell me. Is it seekaret?"

"All our military movements are secret."

"Seekaret? Seekaret?" he screamed, making it sound like "cigarette".

In order to divert his line of thought I took a cigarette out of the packet on the table, and put it in my mouth. I was longing for a smoke.

He was furious. Leaning over the table, he snatched it out of my mouth and threw it on the deck.

"I am sorry," I said. "I thought you said cigarette."

His line of thought was broken, but after a pause we went through it all again. I thought the only thing to do was to be strong now as his patience was greater than mine and he could obviously wear me down in time. I was tired, dirty, thirsty and empty. He had everything at his disposal. I had nothing.

"I do not know anything about American soldiers in Java, and if I did I would not tell you."

"You no speak. I take you on deck. Fire, fire! Down, down!"

I made no reply. I was wondering what I would do if he did. I thought that the only thing to do was to frighten it out of him. I decided there and then that if it came to a firing squad on the forecastle I would ask for my officers and men to watch the proceedings.

I was getting very sweaty now and a cold feeling ran down my spine. He was watching every movement, like a cat watching a mouse, reading my very thoughts as I think some Japanese can. They are trained from birth to hide their feelings in their faces. We are not. Besides, I for one always show mine, and these at the moment were not particularly palatable to my interrogator.

"Is it still seekaret?"

"I cannot answer your questions."

He turned and rang a bell. An officer came down the ladder, knocked and entered. He handed some signals to the Captain, who spoke to him in Japanese. The officer acknowledged and left. I heard him go up the ladder. I was feeling very sweaty round the collar. Then I heard footsteps of several men marching along the deck going on to the forecastle. I wondered if it was a big bluff or whether it was in earnest. Somehow, I felt that he was not the type of ruthless bully expected of Nazi or Japanese soldiers. This man was a sailor with some years at sea behind him. His ship was obviously well disciplined and well-controlled. No one had put a hand on us yet and their whole conduct had been strictly within the accepted rules of war. We would not have acted much differently, except that we would have interrogated men sooner, before they had recovered from the shock.

He was reading the signals, running his finger down the characters as he read. Eventually, he turned to me and said:

"We have been very humanitarian. Japanese cruisers have saved another 360 of your friends. Also your Captain and Commander."

This was excellent news. The signal he was reading was obviously a report from the rescue ships.

"They will arrive tomorrow morning," he added and I wondered if this was to soften me up, to give a friendly air to the proceedings.

"You say orders still seekaret?" he repeated.

"Yes."

He got up. "Come with me." I did not feel very bright. He made me go up the ladder first and then followed. I was glad to get into the fresh air again, out of his hot, stuffy cabin. Just forward I saw Brougham sitting at a table opposite the First Lieutenant of the ship. Brougham looked a bit wan. He obviously had been through much the same as I had.

I was taken to the after end of the forecastle and left there while the Captain spoke to his Number One. I caught Brougham's eye and he shook his hand horizontally under the table, as if to say, "Not too good, this." I nodded assent.

Then, as there appeared to be no other hope, I decided to play my trump card. Leaving his Number One, the Captain came up near to me. He put his slit, beady eyes close in front of my face, and, hissing like a snake, he said:

"Is it still seekaret? You not speak?"

"No. It is contrary to the traditions of my country and my service."

I looked him square in the face at my full height, standing to attention rather arrogantly like a German in the S.S. That was the trump card. It could only be played once.

He paused a second, then turned on his heel, walked aft and passed through the door and down the ladder leading to his cabin. I never saw him again.

The First Lieutenant beckoned me over. When we beckon, we pull our fingers or hand towards us. They do nearly the opposite. They shake their hand in a manner which almost indicates "go away". I nevertheless realised that he wanted me to join him. There was a third chair and he told me in good English to sit down. Then, taking out a packet of cigarettes, he gave us each one and lit them. He was very friendly and cheerful.

"You two good officers," he said. "You no speak."

We looked at him in amazement and with considerable relief. They had tried a bluff and were quite prepared to lose.

He then asked me if I would like something to eat. I said that I was very thirsty and had had very little to drink for some time and would like some water. He called a sailor and gave an order. The man went away and then returned with some iced water. I drank three tumblers straight off. It was delicious and one of the best drinks I had ever had. The First Lieutenant went off to do something with the hands and left us together smoking and drinking our water. Brougham told me the sort of questions he had been asked - it was very much the same as my interrogation, and he too had refused to admit he knew anything, though he was also getting a bit hot round the collar towards the end of it. Only his interrogator's English was much better than the Captain's and he was not so easily diverted.

Actually they had no intention of using any force on us; I am certain of this now. They just tried to get some answers. If we had acquiesced, so much the better; if not, well they would obey the accepted code of war. Which suggests that their first line Navy in the early months of the war carried out a policy of strict adherence to International Law. Their entire conduct was correct throughout these first few days when we were under the control of their regular naval officers.

Immediately the action was over they had picked out of the water as many of us as they thought safe to carry, and later, after fuelling, their admiral had taken his cruiser squadron and destroyers back into the battle area deliberately to pick up the remainder. Altogether 714 officers and men of H.M.S. *Exeter* were saved and went into captivity as a result. We never found out who that admiral was, though we tried hard; they would not tell us as they thought we were trying to find out his name in order to get something on him.

I have never been able to confirm the name of the destroyer. It began with "N" and I think it was *Natugumo* which means "white clouds of summer".

2

The Lost Lunch

About six o'clock that evening, we saw a hospital ship coming into harbour. We recognised her at once as the *Op ten Noort*, a converted Dutch liner, which we had seen in Soerabaya. She had sailed on the morning of February 28th, to pick up survivors after two Dutch ships, *Java* and *De Ruyter*, had been sunk. The Japanese had obviously captured her at sea, which we thought a bit off-hand, but we were glad to see her as we hoped to get our wounded over to her.

Darley was very bad by this time and I did not think he would survive the night. However, our doctor, Wyatt, thought he might, though he could do nothing for him without medical supplies of any kind. And Wyatt was right. Three months later you would not have known that Darley had even been burnt. He had a new face and was as right as rain. He lived right through the captivity and arrived back in England safe and sound.

Shortly after the *Op ten Noort* had anchored, a landing craft with a ramp forward came alongside and about a hundred men and all the officers were ordered into it. Shoving off, it proceeded to a Japanese minelayer and went alongside.

The officers of this ship were sitting in basket chairs round a table in the centre of the iron deck, while the sailors stood looking curiously at us from the guard-rails. One of the officers said in English that the senior officer was to come aboard. I clambered on board and was conducted to the table. The landing craft then shoved off and proceeded towards the hospital ship.

At the table I found the Captain standing, a really small man, barely five feet in height, in a spotless white tropical uniform, with white socks and bedroom slippers. He reminded me of a dressed up circus monkey. He said in very good English, "How do you do? Please sit down."

Two officers sat down too, and a third was called; the first two obviously did not speak English, as the third interpreted everything that was said for their benefit, as well as for the sailors who had closed round in a circle within earshot. They were very curious, looking at me as if I were a strange creature from another world, and I am not surprised. My appearance was, to say the least of it, bizarre. My hair was uncombed and matted with oil fuel, my face unshaven, my white tropical shirt stained as were my grey flannel trousers which I wore in action as a protection against flash. I had no socks or shoes. They seemed particularly amused by my height and kept putting their hands above their heads to indicate how much taller I was than any of them.

The Captain was charming. He had been assistant naval attaché at Shanghai some years before and knew a number of R.N. officers both by name and reputation. He laughed at everything that he said or I said; it was a way of hiding his feelings in his face.

He produced a bottle of Australian brandy as well as some sweet gingerbread. I was nervous at first about the brandy, thinking it might be doped, but as the officers also drank it I thought I had better do the same so as not to give offence and upset them. It was raw stuff, and I was in no state to be able to carry alcohol, so I lashed my peg with copious amounts of water.

The little Captain obviously was not a very good officer; my guess was that he had been passed over for promotion and had been given what appeared to be an inferior command for his rank. The ship was slack and untidy, the men slovenly and lacking in discipline. He appeared to think that all war-like operations were now over in South-east Asia and the great Nippon was mistress of all she surveyed. He told me of prisoners taken by the thousands in Singapore, Celebes, Philippines, and now Java. As the landings on Java had taken place only thirty-six hours before, I was certainly not prepared to accept such gloomy news.

He asked about the action. When I said that four cruisers and six destroyers were a bit too much for our little group, they all roared with laughter. It was the best joke they had heard for years, but when

H.M.S. Exeter firing at aircraft in Banka Strait, January 1942

I mentioned the very heavy bombing in the Gaspar Strait on February 15th, the day Singapore fell, they laughed even more.

Meanwhile the Captain had been drinking brandy after brandy neat, while the others were doing not too badly either. By filling up my own glass with water, I managed to keep level with them. The Captain had eight claret glasses of it while I was there, about three-quarters of an hour.

I then suggested I should go and see how my men were getting on in the hospital ship, to which all were being transferred, so the boat was called away for me and came alongside. The Captain, by now quite drunk and rocky on his feet, could only manage half the distance from the table to the gangway, which was abreast the bridge. He said good-bye, shook hands and told me to go in the boat, and his officers saw me off more as a visitor and curio than as a prisoner. No guard went in the boat. It just took me as if on a normal trip.

On board the hospital ship, I found general confusion. Everybody was milling round not knowing where to go. A strong guard of some fifty Japanese sailors had been sent on board, armed with rifles and bayonets. They got rather fed up with the turmoil and started being rough, using their fists, rifle butts and bayonets. Actually, they were getting frightened. Logically, they considered it safer to have everyone sitting down than standing up, and they proceeded to enforce it, while our men were not used to being ordered round by Japanese, let alone being assaulted. Some ugly scenes nearly occurred but we just managed to keep the situation in hand. We were to meet this sort of thing for the next three and a half years.

The Dutch officers were so worried about their capture, which was of course quite illegal, that they would do nothing to help. If anything they appeared to me to be rather anti-English, partly I think due to the fact that they blamed the whole position in the East Indies on our loss of Singapore.

There were several nurses on board, most of them volunteer Dutch women from Java. They were splendid. They worked untiringly for the sick and wounded and greatly helped to keep the peace between the British and their own men folk.

When we were made to sit down on the deck, someone put his hand on my sunburnt left foot and the whole top just burst, leaving a great raw area of flesh with no skin. It was very painful and coming as it did at the end of a very trying and fatiguing day, made me feel rather sick. One of the nurses came up a little later and took me into the operating theatre and dressed it for me. While she was doing this, I suddenly felt very queer and faint, and started panting. I was covered in a cold sweat. After a bit I recovered and said I thought I ought to rejoin my men, and make more room for others requiring attention. I remember she gave me an apple which seemed, I thought, rather incongruous at the moment. After the gingerbread and brandy I did not want it, so I gave it to a sailor, who ate it ravenously.

I then realised that we must be very hungry and approached the Dutch master to see if he could provide some food. He refused and said the guards had ordered him not to give any food to the prisoners. This I did not believe. I could not help feeling it was prompted somewhat by a policy of appeasement.

Eventually, at about 10 p.m., they put all the officers into a ward on soft mattresses, and all the men down below in the holds between decks. It was good to be able to lie and on something soft and most of us fell asleep almost at once.

I remember turning to one of my neighbours and saying, "Look at those guards there. They've got rifles and bayonets."

"What of it?" he asked.

"It is a nasty thought, but we are going to look at those continuously from now on till the war is over."

He did not reply.

We woke next morning to the sound of destroyer fans and looking out of the scuttles, we saw a Japanese destroyer coming alongside crammed with survivors. Everybody was shouting out the names of those they could see.

A short time later they came on board. The Captain entered our ward first. Everybody started clapping quite spontaneously, and he stood there quite overcome by our sincere appreciation of having him amongst us. Actually I think he was equally pleased to see us too - the loss of a ship at any time is a great shock to a captain, and the thought of casualties among his crew always the worst part of it.

Some of this second lot were very tired. They had been twenty-six hours in the water. Mark Kerr, the lieutenant in charge of the quarter-deck turret, had spent nearly all of it swimming round putting others on to rafts and timber. He was almost out. They all went to sleep at once, and Mark slept almost continuously for about four days.

At midday, after thirty hours without food, we got our first meal - a ball of very unappetising rice. In the evening, there was something similar but not much. Having recovered from the shock of sinking and capture, we were now assailed by the gnawing pains of hunger, and from this moment it never left us for the next three and a half years. To anyone who has never experienced what being really hungry means rather than having a sharp appetite, it is quite impossible to describe. And it is never forgotten. The sight of a hungry person always fills me now with intense compassion, and moreover I can never bear the thought of any food being wasted.

We remained in this ship in Bandjermasin for the rest of that week. In the ward the officers had a modicum of comfort - mattresses to lie on. Except for half an hour on deck every day, we spent most of the time sleeping, or playing cards with the few packs the nurses had given us, or just gazing into space. It did not seem strange to us to be separated from the men; we expected it as we always do the same with any prisoners we take. So we were unaware of the developments taking place down below where the men unfortunately were herded into a very confined space. Demoralised by defeat, physical exhaustion, hunger, thirst and now extreme discomfort, they were easily suggestible to the sea-lawyer types among them, of which any large group of men contains a few.

We had an excellent ship's company and the officers had got on very well with the men, but once the Japanese had separated them from us it was no longer possible to retain complete control. None of us had imagined for a moment that their attitude towards us could possibly change, yet it did. Officers were definitely not liked in the early days, even months. It was a most unexpected situation and, at first, we took little notice of it. The petty officers also failed to maintain their position and authority.

This led to a feeling which caused, I think, more trouble than any other - the "We're all prisoners of war together" attitude which we first heard in that hospital ship and were to hear for many months to come. The theory was, "We're no longer in the ship, so we don't have to take any notice of the Naval Discipline Act or authority."

From what I have since heard, the same thing occurred in every camp in the Far East, irrespective of the service. It varied of course according to the conditions prevailing, previous standards of discipline and morale, and to the presence or absence of leaders of forceful character, and probably many other reasons too. Later, we were able to restore discipline and we did not suffer very much from its temporary loss. The same cannot be said of all other groups in the Far East, and there are many thousands of graves in the jungles as witness of it. The moral of this part of our story is that a very strict discipline must immediately be imposed on men demoralised by defeat in battle.

A ball of rice and a cup of coffee per day - that was all we had to live on and it was not much. Cigarettes were very scarce. We managed to get a few from the Dutch and Japanese but neither gave very much away, and as we got hungrier our spirits dropped. Hunger is very depressing. The only thing we could do was lie down all day to conserve our strength. Survivors from *Encounter* and *Pope* had arrived with our second group and there were also some from the American submarine, *Perch*.

Every other day, the minelayer came alongside to supply the hospital ship with drinking water as her storage tanks were insufficient for so many people. Sometimes the little monkey Captain used to walk round us in his sword and bedroom slippers, but he eventually gave up coming as we asked too many awkward questions which he could not answer.

On Sunday, March 8th, 1942, we sailed from Bandjermasin, escorted by the minelayer, and arrived the next evening at Macassar in the Celebes, where we anchored in the bay. Then on the day after, the anniversary of our commissioning, we berthed alongside the jetty. The wardroom messman had concocted a marvellous lunch of rice and everything else he could find, and we were about to have it when a crowd of armed guards poured on board and drove us off the hospital ship. The disappointment at missing that meal was indescribable. We nearly wept and were very angry. No amount of pleading and arguing could turn our guards, and from that moment, we hated them.

It was a burning hate, sometimes bursting out in flames, most of the time only smouldering, but always there in our hearts and the gnawing void in our stomachs. In return the guards treated us with malice, sheer sadistic malice, every day from the dawn muster in the morning watch till late at night.

From here on it is the story of that malice, of its intensity, its violence, of the diabolical things it inspired, and of how we re-acted individually or as a group. Its evil purpose was to undermine our spirit to resist by constant starvation and humiliation, by maltreatment and overcrowding, and then to let disease and despair take their toll. Many were to die like branches torn off a tree in a gale, but the trunk being of sturdy oak only bent and did not break. When at last the wind turned, it became a typhoon of nemesis to destroy the Japanese themselves.

They fell us in on the jetty in fives and kept us there for over an hour while they tried to count us. It was terribly hot, the midday tropical sun beating down mercilessly on our bare heads. I was in the second section of fives, while the Captain, to our intense indignation, was in the middle of the officers. We felt that the Japanese should at least have taken him by car.

Eventually we were marched off. We passed through quiet, almost deserted streets with the hated poached-egg flag hanging from every house, which aggravated us and lowered our opinion of the local inhabitants. The few people in the streets watched with a kind of silent intensity. It was terribly degrading, this whole performance of eight hundred British officers and men being marched through the native quarter of an East Indies town by a handful of Japanese guards. Of all my bitter memories this first march stands out as the most bitter, the most humiliating.

Besides, it was agonising - two and a half miles of scorching hot roads which burnt most peoples' feet. I had a pair of backless bedroom slippers acquired from the hospital ship, but I was barely able to walk at all on my raw feet already swollen from malnutrition. We mistook every handsome large building along the coast road for our destination. Each was set against a riot of colourful bougainvillea, but to us this beauty had a garish false note as our hopes sank passing it.

At last we came to a military barracks, entered through the gates and were halted. The whole place was unkempt and dirty, obviously untouched through the monsoon period as the grass on the lawns was about two feet high. We could see hundreds of Dutch prisoners eyeing us from barred windows behind which they had been confined while we were admitted. It was not a very inviting place.

Sixty-three officers were put into the office block of four rooms, while the men went into various barrack buildings designed for native troops. There was nothing in the way of furniture. Just nothing.

Across the road we spotted a number of British prisoners, and by hiding in the doorways so that the guards could not see us signalling, we learned by semaphore that they were from H.M.S. *Stronghold* and the oiler *Francol*. There was one naval officer among them - the only surviving officer from *Stronghold* and a previous survivor from *Prince of Wales*. He was Ian Forbes, a most efficient young lieutenant, who had been sunk three times in three months, apart from once before that in the Norwegian campaign.

The mosquitoes that night were frightful. That torment, with the discomfort of lying on the floor, the fatigue and hunger, made sleep impossible. Besides, the full realisation of our captivity was upon us. We had had a glimpse of the malice. The implications were not encouraging.

3

English-u Number 50

A clerihew by our poetic paymaster describes one of our earliest problems of captivity in Macassar. It runs:

The Far Eastern squat
is not
A dignified pose
For N.Os.

The conveniences, which were designed for natives, were of the squatting type. That, plus the lack of privacy, produced such a psychological effect that most of the officers were inhibited for two or three weeks.

The Japanese authorities had appointed a Dutch lieutenant-colonel named Gortmans to act as the Senior Officer of the camp, which was logical as the Dutch numbered 1,800 to our 945 and the Americans 167. After a few weeks all commanding officers and seconds-in-command of ships, and certain specialists, were drafted to Japan, and so from almost the start I assumed command of all British personnel.

Conditions were far from good. For the first month all we were given to eat was a round bun for breakfast, and for supper a ball of cooked rice with a little green watercress or smelly dried fish. That was all. We made small paper hats or envelopes to hold the rice in as there were no plates.

To allay their hunger men started trading over the fence with the natives, strictly against Japanese rules; and this led to much trouble with the guards and a certain amount of physical violence and judo-throwing.

In the barracks, men were crowded four, sometimes five, to a cubicle eight feet by six without a vestige of bedding or furniture. It was very hot, and you could almost boil water by putting a pan in the sun under a piece of glass. The general discomfort was aggravated by sleeplessness and the lack of clothing resulted in mosquito bites which often went septic.

On the other hand the Dutch were relatively well off. They had boots, uniforms, utensils, mosquito nets and other comforts. They also had money. A few of us were lucky enough to borrow small sums from individuals, but the American Senior Officer and I failed completely as far as our units were concerned. We were informed that there was not sufficient to subsidise our men, but later, when all Dutch currency had to be exchanged for Japanese military paper money, the Dutch handed in 47,000 guilders (over £6,000). On hearing this I re-opened the whole question with the Dutch, and managed to obtain a loan from their Senior Officer acting on behalf of their government. It was paid to the men at the rate of one or two guilders per month, and enabled them to buy such necessities as soap and toothpaste, as well as contraband food, palm sugar in particular.

Morale during that first month sank very low, with discipline rotting away and men doing just what they liked. Our navigator, R.K. Hudson, did some extremely hard work during this period, especially as a liaison with the Dutch, who were suspected of not always being scrupulously fair in the distribution of food. He was a quiet, pious, ascetic officer, who liked solitude, hardship and danger. He had been decorated for service in connection with magnetic minesweeping before joining *Exeter*, and was a volunteer for dangerous service. Before the war he had gone out to Australia before the mast in a full-rigged ship. He assumed that all men could be as honest and upright as himself, and he believed in an atmosphere of informality, preferring to exert his own personality by tact rather than use his rank to keep order among the men. He got all the kicks and none of the halfpence.

I disagreed strongly with the atmosphere of informality. If we were going to survive a long period of captivity, discipline would have to be restored. It is indispensable for morale, and I was determined that we should get back on a proper footing in which officers were respected and obeyed.

One morning, I found a leading seaman loitering outside the galley, a favourite place for scroungers. I told him to go away, but on passing again a little later I found him still there.

"Didn't I tell you to go away?" I said.

"Yes," he replied, without the "sir".

"Aren't you a leading seaman?"

"No. I am a .... prisoner of war. The same as you!"

"Very interesting," I said. "Tell me, are you married?"

"Yes."

"Is your wife drawing your pay allotment?"

"I hope so."

"I hope so too," I replied. "But is she drawing it on the pay of a leading seaman or a .... prisoner of war?"

"A leading seaman, I suppose," he said.

"I suppose so too. Now go away and do as I tell you."

He saw my point, and I never had any further trouble from him. But it was not always as simple as that. My problem was to regain control not of individuals but of a corporate body of some nine hundred men, and I began by going to divisions daily at the evening muster. Men fell in under their own officers as in the ship, thus automatically submitting to authority. In the morning, we fell in by barrack blocks as it was simpler; and as both musters were roughly the same procedure, men started to do in the mornings what they did at night, namely obey the officers and P.O.s of their barracks.

After six weeks, I stopped going to divisions and did both musters by blocks; divisions had played their part and were now out of place. The blocks were composed of a general mixture of all kinds of rates, the P.O.s being in the same cubicles as other ratings; but as there was no point in completely reshuffling the camp, this gradually sorted itself out.

Two ratings refused to co-operate with my policy, and when I ordered them to shift into another barrack for administrative convenience they refused point blank to do so. This was the show-down, the test case, and on its solution would depend the whole future. I took care to speak to them publicly so that all those near-by heard what I said.

"Both of you are to move. This is my order and it will be carried out. You understand what I am saying?"

"We are not going," one of them replied. "We have got our space here and we are staying here."

"I am very sorry, but you will move to the other barrack."

"Why should we? It is no concern of yours where we live and sleep in this camp. The Japanese are in charge."

"That is where we differ. I am in charge of this group, and I intend to see that my orders are carried out. You will move within the next three days."

I then retired to my own quarters. Soon all the British knew of this order and were hanging on the outcome. At the end of the time, they had not moved and were defiant. I sent for them, but they refused to come. So I sent again with a warning that if they did not come I would take the matter to the guards. After some pressure from other officers, they did come to me but their behaviour was anything but respectful.

After some altercation and argument, I decided it was time to close the meeting and said, "I have given you ample warning - three days, but you have blatantly disregarded my orders - gone out of your way to bring me into disrespect. You think I am afraid of you but I can assure you I'm not. I'll give you until two o'clock tomorrow afternoon, and if you haven't moved by then I will report the matter to the Dutch Commandant."

They left, still thinking I was bluffing, and the next day the position was the same. I sent them a message - a last chance to carry out my orders - before I left to see the colonel in ten minutes time. This too they disregarded, so I walked down the road past all our barracks and over to the Dutch quarters. All eyes were on me and it was touch and go; if I had weakened, it would have been fatal as everyone knew that these two had had a fair chance and were asking for trouble.

I reported the case to Colonel Gortmans and insisted that the Japanese be requested to implement my punishment.

The guard petty officer came and listened to the evidence, then asked, "What punishment do you wish these men to have?"

"Seven days in the cells, but no reduction in the food as they do not get enough as it is," I said.

He thought for a while, then replied, "I think five days."

A question of "face" was involved; he must have the final word. It surprised me that he reduced it; with their discipline I expected it to be doubled.

"Five days will satisfy me," I said.

The men were sent for, and this time came without delay. They got a terrible slating from the Colonel, and then the guards took them off.

Fortunately, the Japanese were in quite a good mood that day, otherwise they would undoubtedly have given them a hiding into the bargain. It was a risk I had to take. The whole business worried me as I was loth to put men already confined into worse conditions. Nevertheless, it had a most salutary effect and I never had to have recourse to it again.

Gradually we regained control; anyhow basically. It took a long time for the men to realise that officers were a great buffer between them and the Japanese. After that the whole atmosphere changed and no finer set of men could have been gathered together. The relations between officers and men strengthened throughout and remained so till the end of our captivity. Now years after there are still great ties of friendship between us all, more sincere and loyal than any others I experienced in thirty years at sea.

Our great difficulty throughout captivity was in understanding the Japanese. I had never had any contact with them in my life, never having been out East before. I knew of course of their bad reputation for cruelty and ruthlessness; and in the back of my mind was the idea, born probably of some of the fiction I had read, of our being quietly liquidated by narcotics in cigarettes and that sort of thing. As for "face," I was a novice.

I remember in the early days how difficult it was to distinguish one from the other. They all looked exactly alike to me (I believe we appear equally indistinguishable to them, although I cannot understand why as we vary physically more than they do). Their complexions were all identical - a kind of ochre colour. Their eyes were all dark and markedly slit-shaped. They all had very smooth skins, with no hair on their legs or arms, and on the face only a short and patchy growth. They all seemed about the same height, between 5 ft. 3 in. and 5 ft. 6 in., stockily built, with comparatively broad shoulders, long thighs and very short legs.

I remember asking one of the American officers, who was a qualified Japanese interpreter, whether we uninitiated would ever learn to recognise one from another. He said we should after a short time, and he was quite right. After a few months none of us had any difficulty whatever, nor could we understand how we could have had any in the early days.

This American officer was an expert at Japanese, speaking the language with all its flowery subtleties, and therefore very much respected by the guards who themselves were not of good breeding and education. He could manage them easily as he was very dignified, imperturbable, and adept at masking his feelings from his facial expressions - three factors essential for good relations with Japanese.

It was he who gave us many hints about "face" and their likes and dislikes. One of the things he told us was that we must never refer to them in their hearing as "Japs". Japanese was the correct word to use. "Japs" they considered derogatory.

I did not realise that they did not call their own country Japan, but Nippon. "Japan" is the Chinese word for the characters depicting "The Land of the Rising Sun". We certainly got to know the word "Nippon" by the time we finished with them; actually, it is a word which can very easily be used derisively by change of inflexion of the voice. It runs easily off the tongue and from it they soon became known as the "Nips," which seemed to suit them singularly well. We never used the word "Japs" and after we came out of captivity, it was very strange (and still is) to us to hear anyone refer to them as such.

Their rank and file were full of propaganda about the greatness of their country. It was Nippon this and Nippon that. "Nippon Number One" was a great slogan with them. Often we asked them who came next, and they used to say, "Deutcher Number Two, Italia Number Three, Sovietski Number Four, Amerikana Number Five". We then asked them where the English came, and they would say, "English-u Number Fifty". This was always an amusing game with them.

The American officer explained that their language is very difficult, besides being hide-bound with rigid rules of etiquette, marked distinctions in the forms used when addressing inferiors and superiors, and exaggerated formality. A literal translation of high Japanese for "hungry" is "honourable stomach is empty". Most of their words end in a vowel, hence their difficulty in pronouncing words which do not. They get over it, however, by adding a vowel, which was how "English" became "English-u" and they got their favourite catch phrase "English-u no good".

They found great difficulty in our surnames. Mine became Ku-pa, whence "Ku-pa no good" or "Ku-pa Number Fifty" became common sayings in the camp. As the Senior British Officer I was also known as "English-u Number One". This was, of course, quite appropriate as being First Lieutenant of *Exeter* I was already known as "No. 1" and continued to be called so.

The Japanese were proud of their country and achievements and were never at a loss to say so, though in their heart of hearts they were conscious of being a backward people by Western standards. This gave them militarily a slight inferiority complex, though they were convinced they would overcome any such drawbacks by their own personal fighting qualities - their toughness, endurance and contempt of death.

Those that we knew had all been briefed that on no account were they to be taken prisoner. It was all or nothing for them at that time; for no Japanese who had been taken prisoner would have been allowed to return to Japan even if he was liberated or had escaped. They therefore despised prisoners-of-war, and were always making frightful signs to the officers to commit hara-kiri.

I am certain in my own mind that if their drive on Australia had succeeded, all prisoners-of-war would have been transported for work in jungles, mines and deserts, where they would have been treated as slaves till they died. Subsequently they would have been replaced by more white prisoner labour from the occupied territories, until such time as these had been denuded and ready for a purely Japanese colonisation. That was their diabolical plan, and it was not until their advance was stopped that they started to take a little interest in registering and reporting prisoners. That they kept prisoners at all was only due to the fact that their Western allies kept them. The Japanese are slaves to fashion; but they did no more than barely keep us alive.

After the downfall of Italy, they seemed to realise that it was only a matter of time before they too would be defeated, and they made strenuous efforts in their propaganda to boost their spiritual values, even among us non-combatant P.O.W.s. They were very proud of their Kamikazis (Divine Winds) or suicide pilots and wished to know what we thought of them. A number of us senior officers were given twenty-four hours to produce our replies.

Fortunately, one of the more intelligent of our leaders detected their intentions, which was that we should praise the Kamikazis as divinely inspired patriots. We would then have to concede the higher spiritual qualities of their race as against the Allies spiritual bankruptcy but greater material strength. They were preparing their people for defeat, blaming their lack of raw materials, not their strategy or fighting ability. We did not fall into the trap. We replied that our own pilots were not in the least deterred by the possibility of death, but that it was their duty to return from their missions so that they could undertake others, and moreover that from the Western viewpoint the Kamikazis were an uneconomical use of skilled manpower.

They were very annoyed with our answer: indeed we were lucky to avoid reprisals, as they could be childishly vindictive. Once, a sow which escaped from its sty was given corporal punishment and put on three days low diet for disobeying Japanese orders. A pet monkey that made rude gestures at the Japanese Camp Commandant had its swing taken away.

Their childishness was also reflected in the welfare articles which their amenity organisation sent them. Most of these were toys you would not give to a Western child of eight.

The three principal status symbols sought after by each of our guards were a wrist watch, a screw pencil and a cigarette lighter. Fortunately, considerations of "face" demanded that they should acquire them honestly, so they always paid well when they bought them from prisoners who needed money to buy food. Not that I approved of this policy; and I personally refused to part with my own watch despite some extremely good offers made.

Though we rated less than coolies in their estimation, they could not deny us their respect for the courage and fortitude with which we generally stood up to their worst displays of brutality. Anyone who took a beating bravely and uttered no sound usually got off lighter, while the man who fell down and cried for mercy suffered. The sight of cowardice always brought out the marked sadistic streak in the Japanese character.

Infliction of pain came naturally to them, and they seldom knew when to stop. I recall a native, not a prisoner-of-war, who was punished in our camp for failing to bow to the Nip sentry who traditionally represents the Emperor and must be given formal respect by all ranks including senior officers. The native was beaten almost insensible. The guards then set fire to the hair on various parts of his body and bound him to the railings for the night. Next morning they sent for iodine, ostensibly to dress his wounds. The iodine was highly concentrated - 7½ per cent compared with the usual British solution which is 2½ per cent - but instead of putting it on his wounds they put it up his nose. Then he was locked up for a month.

If maltreating a harmless native gave them pleasure, it was nothing compared with the kick they got out of beating up a white man, something they had never had the opportunity of experiencing before. Quite obviously it made them feel good; and, judging from the things they did to us, they certainly had a wonderful time for the next three and a half years.

After those humans whom they were in a position to punish and punch up without fear of retaliation, their cruelty turned to animals. They kicked and threw dogs around. They poked at caged animals with sticks. They caught small birds and pulled off their wings. And worse. Yet, oddly enough, they were really wonderful with children.

With women they were a curious mixture. In their own country the wife is the husband's chattel, with one main duty - to bear him sons. She is treated as his inferior, one who must be unquestionably loyal to him, while he need not necessarily be loyal to her in return. As a result Japanese males are notoriously promiscuous, more so perhaps than those of any other nation in the world, yet the conduct of their occupation troops in the Southern Regions was almost exemplary in regard to women.

Cases of rape were practically unknown; although of course this merely illustrates the level of their discipline, as such excesses were strictly forbidden, rape in particular being punishable by death. On the other hand some of the other atrocities committed by the same troops are almost impossible to believe.

Some people find it difficult to understand why prisoners-of-war did not react to violence by retaliation, regardless of the consequences. It would have been senseless to do so, as it would, without doubt, have led to most savage reprisals. It was never out of our minds that they were deliberately provoking us in order to create an incident which they could use as an excuse to liquidate us all. And there were hundreds of sick who were not in a position to defend themselves.

4

The Hair Question

It took the Nips six months to get our camp anything like organised. They are slow at this sort of staff work, being stupidly logical and over bureaucratic. The area was under the control of the Japanese Navy, and the occupying troops came from their naval landing force.

These were specially trained troops for use in assault landings, and were dressed like seamen or in a light shade of jungle green with naval insignia. They were very versatile men and understood seamanship as well as land fighting. They could all ride horses. Many were also trained to speak the rudiments of the language of the country in which they were to fight. Their N.C.O.s were ruthlessly efficient, the men not so good; though their best troops were certainly not used as prison guards.

Very slowly they produced some clothes of a sort, a little more food and equipment to cook it in, some utensils to eat with and off, some sleeping mats and even a few blankets. But they did not produce any nets against mosquitoes, and as a result malaria became the scourge of our camp. In less than two years 96 per cent of the British prisoners still alive had the recurring forms of it.

The Nips insisted on two musters a day, but it was left to unit commanders to carry them out and report. Curiously, our captors themselves seemed incapable of being able to count, and in any case were never quite certain where various people were meant to be. They organised a few working parties of which we provided about a hundred men every day. These were popular, as they enabled men to get outside the camp, where they usually managed to buy food, or otherwise obtain some from the natives. No officers were allowed out.

The Nips were bad at organising working parties of this sort. It was quite common for them to have fifty men told off to move a piano, but only eight to lift a diesel engine into position. Time meant little to them; they often took days over a job which could have been done in hours. We did not mind of course - indeed we made those jobs take even longer if necessary.

Their officers did very little except feather their nests. They just gave orders and left their N.C.O.s to carry them out. In our camp the Commandant was a warrant officer called Nagatomo Shoi; "Shoi" being his rank which they always put behind the name. Nagatomo was not a bad fellow, but so lazy as to be virtually unapproachable. He had been in the service for a long time and away from Japan since 1937. For his long service and good conduct he was given a P.O.W. camp to look after and from it make what he could. Japanese officers like him did not get a pension and were expected to make sufficient by "squeeze" while on foreign service to keep them in retirement. Had he made only one cent per day per man it would have earned him over £1,400 a year. We worked it out later that he made ten times that amount.

One of my earliest recollections of him was when he came one day to a meeting of unit commanders while we were all sitting round the table. The first thing he did was to take two objects from his pocket, throw them on the table and ask what they were. The first object nearly gave us heart failure - it was a detonator; the other was a small green chilli.

It was explained to him what the detonator was, and that if it were not taken away in cotton wool it might blow up the whole lot of us. That lost him "face" as everyone grinned sheepishly. He then asked about the chilli. The Dutch colonel said it was very good food, very pungent but full of vitamins, and he asked if we could have some for the rice. At this, Nagatomo picked up the chilli and bit the end off. He chewed it tentatively, then suddenly his face became so distorted he might have eaten the detonator, and we expected the explosion to occur at any moment. However, Gortmans with great presence of mind, quickly picked up the chilli and bit off the other end saying, "very good" in Malay. Having been made to look foolish once, the Nip could not admit a second defeat. He had to stick it out as best he could. Then he hurriedly left the meeting, without doubt to put out the fire in his burning mouth with copious draughts of water.

According to their practice, any Japanese unit that captured a town or area had the right to make what they could out of it, and our Nips in Celebes milked it nearly dry. It was astonishing what they shipped out of Celebes during the first year of the occupation. You would have expected their limited shipping to have been filled with such war priority materials as nickel, oil, rice, copra, tin - all of which the islands possessed in abundance. They did ship large quantities of these, but at the same time a considerable amount of space was taken up with loot of quite useless value in war.

All the Dutch houses, shops and go-downs were stripped of things like wireless sets, refrigerators, furniture, gramophones, fountain pens, watches, clocks and clothing, which were sent to Japan. Our men used to load them, and the cargoes they packed sounded quite crazy. I remember hearing that in one ship they put ammunition, copra and rice all in the same hold, and finally on top of that they stuck a steam roller.

The sailors naturally did everything they could to load ships badly or dangerously. Plugs in drums of petrol were loosened and then stowed upside down. Rice bags were slit along the bottom with razor blades after being stowed flat. Fragile things like wireless sets were handled with anything but care.

While looting the countries they had conquered, the Nips were proclaiming the formation of their "Greater East Asia Co-prosperity Sphere". This struck us as odd, to say the least: because, if you are building an empire, you put things into it, not take things out.

Even in 1942 this policy of theirs gave me the impression that secretly they felt that eventually they would be driven out of the occupied territory, and were wasting no time in taking all they could before it was too late. This I think was one of the greatest mistakes they made, and was one of the reasons why we never doubted we would beat them in the end. Actually, I think we were all inclined to be over optimistic. Some people were confident we would be out in six months. I always told men, not less than eight months, not more than eighteen. Anyone who talked of 1945 was shouted down as a pessimist. It was just as well. Our wishful thinking gave us hope. We had precious else through those long and miserable years.

After five months, they started to organise work for prisoners on a fairly full scale. Their theory was that every man must work in order to have the honour of eating; that it was the primitive law of life; and that any man who could not work was a liability on those who could. Sickness meant nothing to them; it was uneconomic, so those who were sick, because they could not work, got half rations. It was not the law of life; it was the law of the jungle.

The staff officer at headquarters who dealt with P.O.W. camps was a Lieutenant-Commander Ota, or Ota Shosa in the Japanese form. He was a regular naval officer, who spoke English and Dutch fluently and was a very intelligent and educated person. He had been Naval Attaché in Java before the war, but had not been treated very respectfully by the Dutch during that period. So now was his chance of getting his own back, and believe me he made the most of it. He was as nasty a piece of work as you would wish to meet - cruel, vindictive and quite ruthless. He was also uncertain and two-faced, and therefore really dangerous. In the early days, he appeared quite pleasant and even helpful. In response to a request, he had 1,200 English books collected from Dutch houses and sent up to the camp. They proved a godsend in the years to come.

I had many interviews with him and two interrogations. The latter were not particularly embarrassing, and I managed to avoid any awkward situations. That was when his opinion of the British was just a shade higher than that he held for his pet aversion, the Dutch. But after the battle of the Coral Sea, early in May 1942, he was never the same towards us and he became progressively nastier as time went on.

Once, when he held a meeting of unit commanders, he began by saying, "All men must work. All with technical ability will be employed technically. All others as labourers. That includes you, Colonel."

Colonel Gortmans was never a friend of mine, nor of the British for that matter. But he was a brave man and on this occasion he just laughed in Ota's face. It was a bold and defiant action, and good to see.

Another time, an American naval officer and I were arguing with Ota, trying to get some alleviation of our rigorous conditions. We quoted the Geneva Convention and International Law. He just turned to us and said, "Don't talk to me of International Law. There isn't such a thing. You are now part of the Japanese armed forces, but lower in status that the lowest coolie."

He then ordered us to produce lists of all men with technical ability. We remonstrated about employing P.O.W.s on war work but he only repeated the bit about our status. In the end the lists were duly produced. It was no use concealing such ratings as artificers, as they knew we had them in ships, and in any case could easily have found them out, so we did the next best thing - we slashed down the number. We excluded several categories such as stoker petty officers and chief stokers, so that out of nine hundred men we only gave them fifty-seven. Besides, a number of these were quite bogus as technicians and were only likely to make a mess of any skilled work.

Eventually the Nips took another one hundred and fifty non-technicals from my contingent and from the Dutch and Americans to make up a draft of one thousand. These were all shipped north to Japan in the *Asama Maru* on October 14th, 1942 to work in shipyards.

We had a bad scene with Ota on June 5th, 1942. I remember the day well as it was my thirty-third birthday. Ota had ordered a mass inspection of all men with all their belongings. Nothing was to be left in the barracks. We did not have much in the way of belongings, so it was easy enough.

When Ota came down the road to our section I breezed up rather jauntily and said, "Good morning," taking care not to add a "sir" or even stand to attention. He was obviously in a bad mood, his face stern and his slit-eyes nearly closed. He was large for a Nip and very solidly built.

He said, "Today I come here not as your friend, but as a Japanese officer on inspection. One of the Hollanders did not treat me with the proper respect, so I strike him."

This I thought ominous, as it proved to be, for he immediately insisted that all men should stand properly to attention with their fingers straight down. I tried to explain that we did not do it that way, but with the fingers half clenched.

"You must do it the Japanese way."

"But my men do not understand your way. They have not been taught that way."

"They must be taught the Japanese way, and they will be taught now."

With that he shouted to the guards, who then went round kicking men's hands to make them put their fingers down straight. Even Ota did the same, a most undignified performance for a Lieutenant-Commander and a "Japanese officer on inspection".

They punched a few people in the face, poked into the various collections of gear, and snooped round the barracks, but they found nothing. The trees and bushes were full of contraband. One Nip later on, when Ota was out of sight, shook a tree and a shower of palm sugar rained down. He did not do anything about it. He thought it was rather a joke. If Ota had found it the guards would have caught it too.

That evening, I had my beard off to celebrate my birthday. It was my first beard, three months old by then, well clipped and pointed. But I loathed it, and one of the ratings who had "acquired" a cut-throat razor removed it. I cannot describe how wonderful it felt having a smooth face again.

John Hickley, the First Lieutenant of *Encounter*, had started the clean-shave fashion and it spread fairly quickly among the officers. Men followed suit. It was astonishing what a boost this was to morale, now that we had got over the initial shock of our set-back and had settled down to captivity. But soon the whole hair question was to loom up large in importance. It was to play a vital, even a tragic part in the existence of the British in Macassar.

In August, a party of British were sent out to Maros, about fifteen miles away, to build an airstrip. It started with one hundred men but gradually worked up to four hundred. The conditions here were pretty poor but many men liked it being free from the confinement of a prison camp, though it proved a most unhealthy spot as malaria in particular was very bad there. In addition the poor diet men had lived on for our first six months in captivity had seriously undermined their health, and the strain of the extra work soon laid them low. They went down with dysentery, beri-beri, pellagra, dengue, leg ulcers. They had to work and sleep in one pair of shorts and jacket, and having practically no soap helped in no way towards their physical fitness.

There were no officers in this party, so welfare and discipline had to be controlled by ratings, and four rose magnificently to the occasion. There was an E.R.A., R.C.F. Chandler, nicknamed "Chilli," who was in charge for over two years and did a first class job, a fine example of leadership. He was supported by Chief Writer T.F. Dunbar, Sergeant B.J. Preece, and P.O. Airman E.W.J. Blackwell, the three Musketeers as we called them.

These four had their work cut out handling not only unpleasant guards but their hungry and spirited men whom they had to protect from the machinations of the Nips. They also took good care to see that the work was done as slowly and unsatisfactorily as possible. I heard later that the airstrip was so sited, relative to the prevailing winds, that most aircraft that landed there overshot the strip and ended up in the coconut palms.

The departure of the Maros party eased the accommodation in the camp at Macassar, but so many returned to us sick that we had to send reliefs at the rate of fifty per fortnight to replace them. The result was that the British in the camp became almost entirely composed of sick men, which annoyed our local authorities who were continually demanding more hands for working parties than we had available.

In July 1942, the Nips started to tighten up its discipline generally, continually punishing men for offences against their rules. There were some terrible beat-ups carried out mostly by a savagely sadistic guard named Yoshida. Ota haunted the camp, fussing about the technical party earmarked for Nippon, and very worried that there might be adverse criticism from the homeland if the party did not appear up to Nippon standards. He went about insisting that the prisoners should learn the Nip salute, not unlike our naval one, and their bow when uncovered. The latter was a hideous thing of which we all had the greatest dislike.

In the middle of all this three Dutchmen escaped one night and were missed at the morning muster. From the Nips' reaction it was quite obvious that there would be serious repercussions on the rest of the camp. The men concerned were a sub-lieutenant, a naval P.O. and an army sergeant. Our feeling generally was "Good luck to them," though we did not think the escape opportune at the moment, as the natives were known to be hostile to white men, and with the monsoon blowing from the south-east a sea voyage to Australia, the nearest friendly territory, would be long and difficult.

That evening they were brought back into the camp with their hands bound behind their backs. The Camp Commandant had taken out a platoon of guards to bring them in, and he was tired, dusty and in an ugly mood. Moreover he had had an awkward interview at headquarters with Ota, who held him responsible. The culprits were not in a good physical state, having been badly beaten up by the guards. One was bleeding from the head and all of them had blood stains on their shirts. They were thrown into gaol still bound.

Meanwhile all who had shared the same cubicle as the officer, plus those within twenty feet of the sleeping berths of the ratings, had been arrested and confined in two large cells. There were about twenty of these and they were considered as accomplices.

The next afternoon unit commanders were sent for by Gortmans and told that all men in the camp were to have their hair clipped. This came as a ghastly shock as the thought of looking like convicts was distasteful to us. Then Yoshida came down with Mori, the senior P.O. of the guard, and said that this was to be done at once. We haggled for some time, and the Colonel who said that the only way to take such an order was to make a joke of it, showed us how by putting on a comedy act in front of the Nips, roaring with laughter and cutting bits of his own hair off with scissors. He then got the Dutch interpreter to clip his hair off, all the while keeping up his ridiculous buffoonery which to my mind impressed the Nips neither one way nor the other.

I for my part strongly disagreed with the Colonel in his handling of the situation. Plainly there were two reasons for the order. First, it was a security measure to prevent any further escapes; you cannot grow a head of hair overnight. Secondly, it was an excuse to reduce us to their own common denominator, making us follow their own military custom since, by their own assertion, we were part of their armed forces.

As they were not particularly pressing about the hair business at the time, I took no action that day, though many of the Dutch started doing it which annoyed us as it spoilt our chances of standing out against it. When I told our people about the hair they were angry, and strong pressure was brought to bear on me to prevent our being thus further degraded by the Nips.

For the next day or two various conferences of Japanese staff officers met in the camp guardhouse, where the accused were interrogated to reveal their plans and their contacts outside the camp. It transpired that they had escaped at midnight by getting over the fence into the adjoining native village, having left their mosquito nets down to give the impression that they were still inside.

They had walked about nine miles during the night, to a remote creek where they had a boat arranged with an outside contact. But they had made the mistake of not hiding from the villagers after daylight, thinking they would be loyal. They were not.

During the afternoon while loading their boat with food, the Dutch were surprised by a party of Nips who had been tipped off by some natives. Unfortunately, one of the three had a gun on him, a fatal thing to be found with during an escape; but suicidally stupid in this instance as he had no ammunition.

Meanwhile the hair problem was becoming more complicated. I had asked Mori, the No. 1 of the guard, whether we need do it. I told him that the white men could not stick the sun in the tropics without hair, especially as we were without hats. I said we would get sunstroke; I honestly thought so at the time, but it proved later to be utter nonsense. He said that he thought we ought to do it but actually did not mind one way or the other. Yoshida on the other hand was determined that we should.

I eventually made what I consider to be my greatest error of judgement as the Senior Officer of the British. I decided to press the views of my compatriots, to try to hold out against the order. It was a terrible pity, as we never really recovered from this unfortunate mistake. I went to the Colonel and asked him to see the Nips about it again. I also spoke to the Dutch interpreter. Both said the moment was inopportune as the Nips were in a bad mood about the escape.

Next day I tried again, and this time the Colonel said that he was having difficulty with the Nips about the punishment to be meted out to those who had escaped. He said he was fighting for their lives. This was the first time that I was made aware of the possibility of their being condemned to death, and, since there was a far greater issue at stake than our appearance and our dignity, I said no more.

The sentence on the escapees remained pending for many days. Doubtless the authorities were awaiting confirmation from their superiors regarding their proposed action. The escape took place, on September 7th. By the 11th or 12th the hair question reached its crisis.

Yoshida came prowling round our block one night at about 1 a.m. and found, he said, a man committing a nuisance against the wall. The man denied it; in fact I am sure now that the whole thing was trumped up by Yoshida who had done it himself. A frightful scene ensued, with much shouting and noise, which even David Chubb, my diplomatic second-in-command, failed to quieten.

Yoshida, having finally dropped his charge against the man, next demanded to know why we had not carried out his orders to remove our hair. I replied that Mori had told us that we need not do so.

"But I, Yoshida have ordered you," he said. "You must obey me. I give orders in this camp. No one else."

"But you are only Number Two," I said. "Mori is Number One."

I could not have angered him more if I had spat in his face. Looking back, I realise now that it was a serious mistake and I am convinced Yoshida swore vengeance on me and all the British from that moment.

It was never the same again, and the war he waged on us with ever increasing ferocity in the years to come undermined sick and ailing men, so reducing their resistance that disease smote them down and they died as a result. I hold myself entirely to blame for this.

He ordered us to clip off next day, and, with the fate of the Dutch escapees still undecided, there was not much else we could do but obey. Personally I did not mind very much. Hair would grow again and, having been knocked about publicly pretty often already, I was quite impervious to insults and humiliation. In any case no one is humiliated if he does not wish to be.

All hair had to come off, beards and moustaches included. I led the way to the "barber's" chair and all the officers followed. We looked a comical sight with our bristling blue heads that made our thin faces appear even more haggard than before. When the men came in from work that evening they roared with laughter at us, then at themselves as they underwent the same treatment.

On September 14th, one of our seamen became very ill with cerebral malaria; the doctor told me he was unconscious and could not live, and at 4 p.m. he died. I got the message only a few minutes before a bugle sounded for the camp to fall in. This was an unusual time and obviously something was going to happen.

Having fallen in on the grass square in the centre of the camp, we saw Ota and other officers from headquarters near the gate. After reporting all present, the British and Americans were sent to the coconut grove just outside our quarters and ordered to wait there until Ota came to read a proclamation. We did not understand what this could possibly be but it was obviously going to be something very nasty. You could sense danger or bad news in that camp.

After about ten minutes Ota arrived with some other Nips. A kind of dais was raised for him to stand on. Then, while we all stood to attention, he read us the proclamation.

The original, in Dutch, he had just read to the Dutch contingent, and now he seemed to be translating it into English as he went along.

It ran roughly as follows:

"I am to inform you that on the night of September 7th three Dutch nationals (he named them), while under Japanese discipline, deserted from this prisoner-of-war camp at Macassar. But next day, pity for them, they were taken by Japanese soldiers. The Japanese High Command has decreed they shall be shooted to death. They are satisfied that the officers and men who were billeted in the same room and barracks were not actual accomplices. They will therefore be punished in another way."

Having come to the end of the statement, he merely stepped down from the dais and without a sign of emotion, walked away.

We were then told to fall out, but to my astonishment the men just broke ranks and rushed across to their barracks making rather a noise. There was even some hilarity and sound of laughter. It was rather dreadful, and the retiring Nips looked at them angrily and surprised; and we, the officers, were pretty stunned ourselves. Obviously the men just did not think or fully appreciate the real meaning of it all. Privation and suffering had already made them callous and impersonal to events which did not immediately or directly concern them. In the latter years we officers became pretty callous ourselves; if we had not I feel we would not have survived, let alone retained our mental stability.

Even while the proclamation was being read to the Dutch, the three condemned men were being taken from the cells near the gate to a spot about two hundred yards away, near the sea. There they were beheaded, not "shooted," and buried together without religious rites. However, when the camp was moved over to that area in 1944, their bones were dug up, each victim being identified by a boot or some article of clothing. These bones were put into the coffin of the next man who died and re-buried by our Padre, Gerald FitzGerald.

By this stern punishment the Nips intended to make quite certain that no one else tried to escape. They had so few guards, and so weak an occupation force, that they could not afford the inconvenience and danger of men escaping. To cover their action in inflicting the death penalty they had ruled that the men were under Japanese military discipline. In their own services the penalty for desertion was death.

The room-mates of the executed Dutchmen were locked up for two months, for the first month being kept on a very low diet and allowed no exercise. In October they got camp food and one hour's walk round the camp per day. They were eventually released by an amnesty on the occasion of the celebration of the anniversary of the Restoration of the Meiji, sometime in November. They and the rest of the camp were given clearly to understand that they had escaped execution themselves only by the skin of their teeth, and that in the event of any future escape attempts all room-mates would suffer the supreme penalty, whether the escapees were caught or not.

This was a real deterrent, for though a man might be prepared to risk his own neck, or head in this case, the last thing he wanted was to involve his chums. In any case the chances of escaping successfully were quite hopeless. Most of the natives were hostile, and the few who were not would have had to risk savage reprisals on themselves and their neighbours to harbour any prisoner. Few of us were fit enough to effect an escape and undertake a boat journey in the tropics. We gave much thought to these problems, but they were insoluble.

Ota came one Sunday forenoon to say good-bye to the unit commanders. He told us he was going home to do a staff course and was sorry to bid us farewell. He added that he had been very impressed by the high standard of discipline in the camp.

"I advise you to continue. If you don't the punishment will be very severe."

His parting present to us was a packet of cigarettes, at a cost to him of about sixpence. We were glad to see the back of him.

I often think of him interrogating me one day. He was in a chatty mood in the hope presumably that I might talk and give away information unwittingly. I had a beard at that time, as no one had any shaving gear.

"I think this war will go on a long time," he said. "I think you will be in captivity for many years. Your beard will be very long by the time you are free."

I replied that I was not prepared to agree with him.

"You must remember," he said, hissing unpleasantly, "that from the capture of China and the Southern Regions we have sufficient raw materials to continue the fight against you for ten thousand years."

"In that case my beard will indeed become very long."

He did not particularly like this and the conversation ceased abruptly. He did in fact mean exactly what he said. The Japanese were prepared to fight for ten thousand years if necessary, and personally I doubt whether they regard their recent defeat as anything more than a temporary setback.

5

Yosh

His full name was Yoshida Tomanao, and for those of us who lived under his reign of terror that name is an expression of evil - the evil of sadism, brutality, dishonesty, cunning and inhuman tyranny - evil of a peculiarly Japanese flavour.

For a time he was known to us as "Goldtooth" - he had flashing gold teeth. This nickname, oddly enough, was abbreviated by some to "Goldie", though personally I could never understand how anyone could think of anything that sounded even remotely affectionate for the Nip in question. There were several other names for him too, such as "The Mad Mullah" and "The Yellow Peril," but none of these lasted very long. Soon even "Goldtooth" disappeared and he became just "Yosh".

Who exactly was Yosh? The question has never fully been answered. But to show how he came to dominate our lives in Macassar let me return again to the first few weeks of our captivity.

During that period the only guard who had been at all conspicuous was one named Kakoi, a 2nd class seaman in charge of the galley. But we had noticed that, whenever something happened to annoy the Nips, it was another guard called Yoshida who beat the culprit up, usually with a baseball bat. He wore a yellow armband which seemed to give him greater authority, as far as discipline and working parties were concerned, than all the other guards regardless of their rate or seniority. This seemed very strange as Yoshida at that time was no more than a 1st class seaman (equivalent to our able seaman) from the Japanese landing force which formed the garrison at Macassar.

The Japanese navy did not appear to have any specialist petty officers or seamen. There were just six ranks - 1st, 2nd and 3rd class petty officers, and 1st, 2nd and 3rd class seamen. There were no writers, supply ratings, cooks or anything like that: anyone could be told off to do these jobs and, what was so creditable, was able to do them too. Though trained primarily as fighting men, they were all extremely versatile.

In our camp, senior P.O.s were detailed for the administrative and clerical duties. One was responsible for the records of the prisoners, another for supplies, a third for the records of the guards themselves. Yosh, though below them in rank, wielded the executive power of his armband which was subject, in theory at any rate, only to the No. 1 or guard commander, who was a 1st class P.O.

Actually I believe the yellow armband job should have gone to a senior P.O. Why then did it go to Yosh, a mere A.B.? No satisfactory explanation was ever obtained, and it can only be assumed that he was specially selected for this duty by Nagatomo, the Camp Commandant, who was intelligent enough to realise that the administration of a large prisoner-of-war camp could raise difficult and embarrassing problems and moreover that he had very few guards to ensure security. He was not going to have his career marred at its close by P.O.W.s. In Yosh he had obviously seen a man who could be relied upon to safeguard his interests, and he told him to run the camp in any way he thought fit. So long as there were no awkward incidents, no questions would be asked.

But there must have been more to it than just that, for in practice at least here was a mere A.B. who was very nearly all powerful in the camp. Besides, he was far from being deferential to the officers from Headquarters who visited us. The Japanese are rigidly strict in observing the outward forms of authority in the chain of command, yet we used to see Yosh talking to them with his hands in his pockets.

He appeared to be an average type of regular Japanese sailor. At that time he was thirty-one, about 5 ft. 5 in. in height, very strongly built with the usual wide shoulders, long thighs and abbreviated legs of the Nip. He had very marked slit eyes and thick lips that opened to disclose the most distinguishing feature of his face - his row of flashing gold teeth. He was remarkably fit considering that he chain-smoked, drank hard and, on his own admission, had had V.D. for several years. He had served in Manchukuo, China, Pilau, and had been on a training course in Formosa. He had been away from Japan for nearly five years.

It surprised us that he was not a P.O. as he had several outstanding qualities - courage, dynamic energy, a great capacity for work, exceptional physical endurance, and a gift for improvisation. As a personality he was head and shoulders above any other Nip in the place. What then had held him back? He was known to be weak educationally, but that would not have prevented his promotion as he was far from being unintelligent. One possible explanation was that he was a spy in the ranks for the Kempetai, the Japanese Secret Police. This would explain his highly privileged position. It would also fit in with what Nagatomo wanted. There would be no trouble in the camp as Yoshida would rule by brute force and terrorism. Nor would there be any difficulty with the Kempetai as he was one of them.

From Nagatomo's point of view there must have been few people more perfectly suited for the yellow armband than Yoshida. It was not very long before the entire camp revolved round him. He controlled everything effectively and smoothly, and it was so right to the end, when he went on punishing prisoners even after the capitulation of Japan. The Nip officers from Headquarters seemed to have no control over him, nor apparently, did they wish to as obviously he was a great economic asset. With only seventeen guards besides himself he achieved a trouble free camp of 3,000 prisoners.

Yosh ran the camp on a policy of fear with collective and indiscriminate reprisals for the slightest infraction of rules on any and everybody, whether innocent or guilty, healthy or sick. When anything annoyed him, or he deliberately intended to be unpleasant and trumped up something, he could produce displays of terrifying anger, with sadistic assaults on any individual or group without any attempt at an investigation or giving them a chance to explain.

Terror tactics were often employed. On two occasions, the Padre was sent for, before a man was due to be beaten, and told to read the funeral service over him as the culprit was to be beaten to death. The Padre appeared to comply, but what he actually said to the victim was:

"You don't have to worry - they are only trying to frighten you. But what we can do now is say some prayers."

In a rage Yosh was very dangerous as his passion could only be satisfied if he hit someone, either with his fists, his club or anything handy that came within his grasp. Efforts by officers to mediate more than often resulted in making matters worse, with further victims added to those already attacked, including the mediators themselves.

I used to call him "The Magnesium Flame" - he had only to be touched off to flare up into a white hot fury. But when it had burned itself out he would become quiet, subdued and on occasions even penitent and ashamed. He knew he lost "face" by these scenes, yet appeared unable to help himself.

When he was on the warpath he was very frightening. I have seen five or six hundred British sailors including myself standing stiff at attention, not daring to move an eyelid. A flood of Japanese would pour forth from his tongue; and the sound of this shouting was always the prelude to a scene. At night it was quite eerie and not unlike a mad dog. I doubt that anyone who lived in that camp could ever forget it.

Then would come the beat-up. First the punching in the face, usually with the inside of the clenched fist, to save his knuckles, then always the flogging on the backside with the victim leaning at an angle of forty-five degrees against a wall or tree. Sometimes the victim would be strung up by his wrists tied behind his back with his feet just touching the ground. Yosh was a remarkably good shot and rarely hit off the target area except when he put a special low one across the thighs for spite.

Most of the guards gave a hand in the terrible beatings that prisoners had to endure, but it was Yosh who dealt out the majority. In the early months he used the baseball bat already mentioned - a wicked weapon; but later he devised one that was far worse a club of the same shape, but slightly lighter and about a yard long. If this was not readily available, he soon found a suitable substitute. During a beating it was unwise to utter any sound, as this only inspired the Nip who was administering the flogging to even greater efforts; on the other hand to stick it quietly earned the victim the guards' respect - they would give him the thumbs up sign and say "Good" in Malay.

The great danger was in falling down. For some reason this made Yosh and any guards in the vicinity go quite wild, and they would rush round the victim kicking and stamping on his face and body with their hobnailed boots; they would in fact kick him back into the standing position. Serious injury was liable to be inflicted to the head, spine and limbs. Burst ear-drums were by no means uncommon.

Often before and after a beating the victim would be subjected to judo-throwing. The guards would take turns, and, each time the prisoner, already suffering from the shock of his corporal punishment, staggered to his feet, he would be thrown again. He might be thrown twenty times, but that was not always the end of it. He might then have to go down on the ground in the stoop-fall position - (the position on the hands and toes from which you do press-ups) - and stay like that over extended periods. On one occasion, having broken a man's wrist, Yosh still made him do press-ups.

Other forms of punishment included standing in the sun or doubling round the camp on wooden clogs for periods up to three hours. In addition there were punishments, some of them bizarre, which Yosh thought up on the spur of the moment. Once, on finding a Dutchman up a mango tree in the camp, he ordered that, since the prisoner acted like a monkey, he could stay in the tree all night.

Reprisals were frequent on officers and petty officers in charge of barracks or working parties and inflicted in full view of the men. I myself was assaulted more than fifty times in various ways.

Yosh would wait months to catch people he particularly disliked, so the extent of a beating varied not only with the alleged crime but also with the man. Normally, the number of strokes in a beating would be between twenty and thirty. The maximum was received by one of our stokers who had two hundred and seven with a wooden club. He never uttered a sound and was still standing at the end. Even Yosh was defeated - he was too exhausted to continue. The man was on the sick list for a long time, but he was much respected by the Nips for his courage.

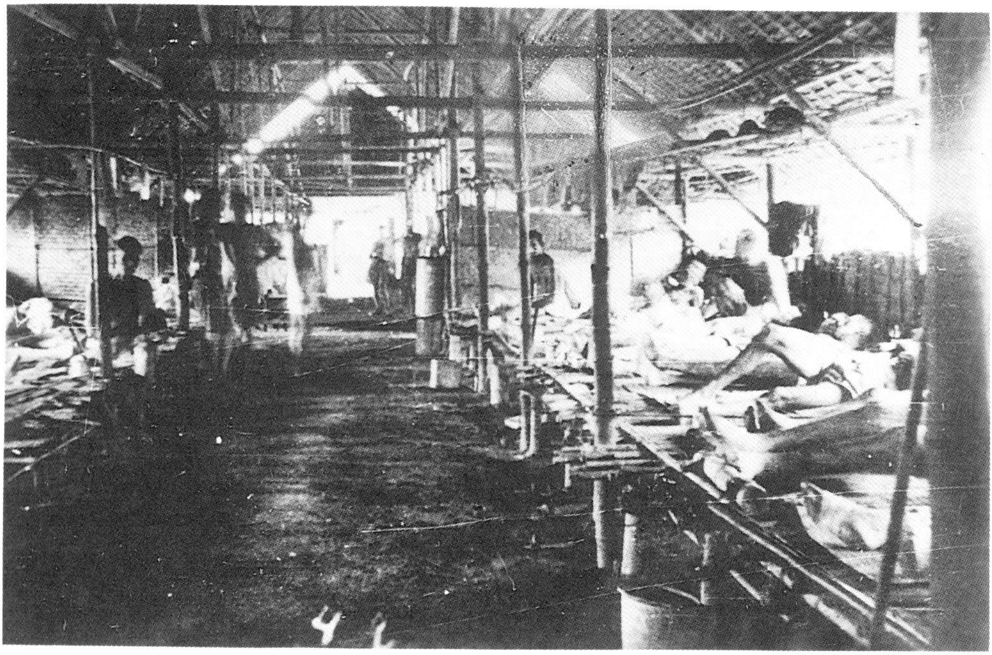

Typical interior of a bamboo hut in a Japanese P.O.W. camp

Men on working parties were frequently beaten by guards on the spot, then reported to Yosh on their return to the camp and beaten again over great welts already extremely painful to the touch. One of the worst of these cases was that of a Dutchman who had thirty-five from a working party guard, and two hours later forty-eight from Yosh. The prisoner was still conscious at the end but pouring with blood; and the doctors had to open him up in hospital afterwards to relieve the frightful bruising.

Some people became partly inured to these nauseating scenes after a time, but they always left me with a sick feeling rather akin to seasickness combined with that sensation you get with a sudden fall. This was brutality of a sort none of us had ever seen before, or even imagined as that which any human being could inflict on another. All the British had been in many air-raids and surface actions and were trained to accept the hazards of war. But this brand of attack on the body was something completely new to them and quite unnerving. Generally in battle a man could fight back, or just take cover, and if he was lucky he had a good chance of not being hurt. But there was no defence against Yosh. If he hit you with that club it was going to be mighty painful, and if you did not manage to stand up in silence it was going to be worse. In any case there was a chance of being seriously damaged for life.

The uncertainty of Yosh's temper meant that we lived on an emotional volcano that was constantly erupting with sudden and horrifying brutality; and to men always hungry and in most cases debilitated by some form of sickness or ailment, ill-clothed and herded in quarters like animals, this ordeal of terror caused a nervous tension from which no one was exempt. This tension was so strong that you were aware of it all the time; and you knew immediately if Yosh had left the camp to go to town.

Undernourishment and malaria reduced one's physical ability to stand up to punishment, while vitamin deficiencies tended to undermine the nervous system making it difficult to withstand the emotional strain of watching violence inflicted on a fellow prisoner. All of which created a permanent sense of insecurity in the camp, and the mental and physical deterioration it caused in later years led to many deaths.

According to David Chubb, who succeeded as the Senior Officer in charge of the British contingent after most of the officers were drafted to Java in October 1943, the situation if anything got worse. Yosh resorted to mass beatings and David reported that whole parties or barrack blocks would be assaulted for the fault of perhaps one man.

"The climax," he says, "was reached in February 1945 when after a sudden search for eggs, illicit sugar, etc., in the barracks, over one hundred and twenty men were badly beaten and the entire camp made to witness the procedure which lasted for more than two hours."

Often a man's health would collapse after a beating. It was as if the pain and shock had lowered his resistance; and though up to that time he may have withstood the major tropical ills, he now went down with one or more of them. One of the common diseases was pellagra, a deficiency disease, the progress of which is controlled to a large extent by the mental condition of the patient. On being frightened and demoralised many pellagra cases lost their mental stimulus and died. They died very easily and very quickly, sometimes within a few minutes of collapse.

Altogether 186 British sailors died in captivity in the Celebes. There can be no doubt that Yoshida Tomanao was one of the main contributory causes of their deaths.

As the only approach to the Camp Commandant was through Yosh, any form of representation or complaint against him would have been spiked at the start; moreover, in the unlikely event of any such complaint being upheld, he would have lost "face" and taken good care to revenge himself on all of us. Had he wanted, he could have made life even less bearable than it was. He could and did stop men's food at times, and he could always take reprisals on the sick. He had the whip hand, and once when a complaint was actually made about unnecessary beatings of a working party, the whole party of thirty were fallen in and accused of making arrogant assertions concerning the future successes of the Allied forces. Those guilty were ordered to step forward. As the charges were false none did so. They were then threatened with digging their own graves and mass execution at dawn, the Padre being sent for and ordered to read them the last rites. They were then locked up in a cell for the night. Next morning they were released and sent out to work and nothing else happened.

Yosh hated me, and this unfortunately reacted adversely on the British. This personal prejudice probably stemmed from the physical inferiority he felt from being nearly a foot shorter than I was, and was increased by my determination not to lick his boots which was what he wanted me to do. Whenever I intervened, or got sent for in a scene, it was like throwing petrol on a fire. This worried me as it was not in the interests of my men, but I think they were prepared to accept the extra suffering I must have caused them rather than that I should adopt a more subservient manner towards the man they loathed and despised. Indeed they assured me of this on several occasions, adding that any assaults or indignities I was made to suffer in their presence could not humiliate me in their eyes. It was a great solace to know they were behind me practically to a man.

The cause of most of the trouble was food smuggling. There were two reasons why we were forbidden to bring food into the camp. The first was a simple one. It stemmed from the Nips' suspicious nature and their exaggerated security consciousness. Buying food from the natives provided the means for us to conspire with them to revolt against the Japanese occupation. Food was an excellent cover for letters, money and even more dangerous articles. It was also a method by which reliable news could be obtained to off-set the censored news and propaganda that reached us from official Japanese sources.

The other reason is far less simple for it is tied up with the inexplicable logic of the Japanese mind and their preoccupation with "face". Doubtless a naval regulation, based on abstruse calculations, fixed the amount of cash allowance for our daily rations. Doubtless, too, these were based on what was considered adequate to keep the average man alive and working. I have no idea of what it should have been - little of it reached us after the Camp Commandant's and probably Yosh's "squeeze" had first been deducted. But the diabolical part of the system was that the Japanese authorities, hide-bound by red tape, were not prepared to make any allowances for this "squeeze". Besides, to have done so would have meant admitting that something was defective or wrong. So whether we were "squeezed" or not, the rule had willy nilly to be enforced.

If the quantity of food that reached us kept us just above starvation level, that salved their conscience. That men should become weak and die was of little or no concern to them.

From our point of view it was essential that the rations should be implemented, and if this could be done by smuggling then this source should be exploited. The sailors found it difficult to eat rice, the basis of our diet, on its own, and the addition of sugar, milk, fruit or eggs made it both palatable and nourishing.

The British were prepared to go to great risks in this smuggling racket. Some men did it simply for the excitement and the sheer pleasure of defeating the enemy. Despite the penalties for being caught, this game kept morale at a high level. Others did it for gain.

At the start the Dutch had all the money, and we had none. However, once our men had managed to borrow some they were in business. With a small working capital they began trading, buying food from the natives, smuggling it in, and selling it at a high profit to cover the risk involved, and within a few months a large proportion of the Dutch money was in British hands. Most of our men had some; but a few were really rich. It was enterprise of a bold, tough, Empire-building calibre.

There were other sources of income. One in particular was that of looting from the Nip go-downs at the docks. Once, a whole bale of coloured singlets was plundered and smuggled into the camp under the noses of the guards and sold at a good profit.

The nerve and ingenuity displayed in smuggling operations are deserving of the highest praise, and the standard of sleight-of-hand practised would have earned the smugglers the approval of a professional conjuror; only that instead of producing things out of a hat - eggs, tinned foods, fruit and improbable necessities like electric light bulbs - they did the opposite.

When the hat trick was finally exposed, and the Nips ordered that people with hats should take them off and hold them upside down on their hands for examination as they passed through the gate, some smugglers beat the guards with sheer psychology. They just held contraband in their hands under the hats. It was such a risky and easily discovered hiding place that the Nips never thought of lifting a hat; their tortuous oriental minds could not grasp the possibility of anything so obvious, and those who had the audacity to try the ruse were safe in its ingenious simplicity.

Other methods consisted of tying foodstuffs to the leg or carrying it in bags in the crutch or armpits. Eggs would nestle in the overhang of a man's shirt. Sugar came in the false bottom built into the gash cart.

Yosh knew that food was being brought in regularly; and he overtly approved as he was logical enough to see that extra food kept men fitter and he could therefore get more work done. But it annoyed him to think of British sailors out-smarting Japanese guards; and he would let weeks go by to lure smugglers into a false sense of security, then suddenly he would pounce and catch them red-handed. He could always use this at any time as an excuse to create a scene to re-instil terror if he thought we were getting slack, or to slake his thirst for revenge when news was bad for the Japanese from the war front, or merely to satisfy his sadistic lust.

Usually the food would be destroyed in the presence of the smugglers, which to men whose bodies craved it was sheer mental sadism. Eggs were invariably smashed in their faces, and the culprits would be made to double round the camp, each holding up some evidence of their crime with perhaps an illicit banana stuck in his mouth.

I would be sent for and the endless arguments through interpreters would ensue. I would pretend to admonish the culprit, starting usually with words, "Take not the slightest notice of what I am going to say to you".

I always assumed the Nips did not understand English; but there was evidence which caused me to doubt whether this was actually so. Once, when Yoshida entered the galley and somebody said, "What's the blighter want now?" he turned and said, "A knife". On another occasion, going round the barracks, he said, "Nasty smell here". To which I replied, "Yes". Then I did a sort of double-take and looked at him.

Was he cunning enough to hide the fact that he understood English, or had he learned a few phrases to give us just that doubt? We never found out.

Yosh threatened many times to take mass reprisals if he found individuals smuggling again, and as this would have caused suffering to many innocent people besides the sick, I had sometimes to ban smuggling operations altogether for a period. However, as soon as I thought I saw the green light again, I let up and risked beatings for the few to help the many.

My chief worry all the time was for the sick, of which we had a continuous average of about one hundred men who were really ill and many more in a debilitated state. Yosh could not abide sick men as they ate Japanese food and did no work in return. His constant grouse was that the sickness rate was too high and the number of hands available for work ridiculously below the camp total. He used to say that he was always in trouble with Headquarters over insufficient working parties.

Yosh suspected men in hospital of being malingerers and that they were only sick to avoid working for him, so he discouraged sickness by making hospital life as uncomfortable as possible for sick people to endure. He used to trump up terrible scenes in the hospital. He would fall in all the patients, regardless of their health and beat up a number of them. Having made them suffer, he would then fall in all those who were sick in barracks and those only fit for camp duty. This parade would last for several hours, while everybody stood in the hot sun.

Malaria and beri-beri cases were forbidden by Yosh to enter the hospital and they just had to stick it out on the barrack floor, so it is easy to imagine how exhausting such a performance was to men with fevers or suffering from nervous exhaustion as most vitamin-deficiency patients were.

It is difficult to understand the attitude they took over the sick, and in this respect particularly the logic behind their policy verged on the insane. Either they wanted prisoners as cheap labour, in which case it was obvious that they should be maintained in a reasonable physical state, or else they wished to undermine them physically to ensure that they could never rise against their captors. They tried to have it both ways.

They allowed the British and Americans to become almost completely infected with chronic malaria before they provided nets, and then gave insufficient quinine to cure it. As Java produced ninety per cent of the world's quinine there was no shortage, and moreover there were ample supplies in Macassar.

They did not provide sufficient food for men to work and this policy of theirs was bound to result in increased sickness. Major policy mistakes of this sort was one of their marked weaknesses in organisation and administration.

Yosh was quite remarkable at times in summing up exactly how fit a man was. He would frequently say, "No good" to a man with a weak heart, when he could not have known his condition by merely looking at him. But there was always a danger that he would select men for jobs which were beyond their physical capabilities, so if unfit men had to go out to work we felt it was better that we did the selection. He knew this, so was able to blackmail the doctors and myself into providing the numbers. This was one of the most diabolical of his tricks against which we had no defence other than guile and subterfuge. Available numbers had to be fudged; men discharged from hospital had to be kept on the sick list; men's identities had temporarily to be exchanged; those with bad heart conditions had to be shown as suffering from something entirely different, usually tropical ulcers, and for which they had to be provided with camouflage bandages. Actually Yosh did not understand any form of internal complaint other than tuberculosis and appendicitis.

Yet, oddly enough, when anyone was very ill or dying, he could be most helpful and kind. He would produce anything we asked for - ice, blankets, liver injections, antibiotics and other drugs. It seemed irrelevant to him that the patient's condition was due to his failure to provide them earlier or to the deliberate policy of his compatriots.

There was one occasion when he was checking our quarterly demand for medical supplies and found we had a figure of 50,000 pills down for quinine. He complained that this was too much, that we had exaggerated views of the extent of malaria in the camp and were doing this to get him into trouble with his superiors. He just crossed off the last nought.

Within a fortnight, we were in desperate need but it took several days of making repeated requests before he eventually realised that the situation was almost out of hand. However, once convinced of our necessity, he jumped on his bike and was off to the main hospital in the town. Some American prisoners who worked there saw him arrive. He walked into the dispensary and demanded quinine. The pharmacist, a Japanese civilian, queried who he was and what authority he had to draw drugs on his own behalf. Yosh just gave him a right hook to the jaw knocking him flat. He took three bottles of quinine off the shelf, jumped on his bike and rode back to the camp.

I remember that he was very pleased with this effort and proudly presented us with the quinine. Naturally we were very pleased too and gave him a big "*Domo Arigato Gosaimas*" (Japanese for "Thank you very much"). He was delighted with his apparent popularity. Conveniently he had forgotten that it was he himself who had previously reduced our demand by 45,000 pills!

Although I considered Yosh the most hateful human being I ever had the misfortune to encounter, I could not but be impressed by his truly outstanding efficiency. To begin with he arranged working parties so that he kept most of the skilled men back to work for the benefit of the camp, and with them organised shops for tailors, cobblers, clogmakers, tool-makers, basket-makers, hut-builders and a dozen other trades.

He himself could turn his hand to literally anything. The variety of his accomplishments in our camp included the complete lay-out and construction of air-raid shelters, turf covered pill-boxes for sentries at strategic points, modifications to the galley, the building of hospital wards, and the sinking of a concrete pool for a crocodile. He was equally at home organising a big parade for an admiral's visit, a funeral, or the daily muster. He knew exactly what he wanted and he got it. There might be some face-slapping, but only to accelerate the proceedings; remember out of three thousand prisoners only two spoke his language, while he could only communicate with the rest in very low Malay. But he rarely failed at any job, and his solution to a problem was nearly always the best answer to it.

In a short while he had made the camp a show piece. It was spotless, with clipped lawns and grass verges, flower borders, vegetable gardens, pigsties, stables for horses, fastidiously tidy barracks, clean and well organised galleys, running water, neatly stacked fuel, electric lighting. He was proud of his camp and curiously of his prisoners; although he hated us, he was faithful to us after his own fashion - he would have defended our honour had any other Nip ever dared to suggest we were not the best prisoners anywhere in the Far East.

Because he worked unceasingly himself he disliked officers. His own tended to be lazy, a quality he could not abide, and we, according to Japanese regulations, could not be sent out of the camp on working parties. To beat the regulation he found work for us to do inside the camp. We were put to cutting grass by hand, tending the gardens, doing daily P.T., scouring our own quarters and a hundred other chores. He hated to see any of us doing nothing, and it was highly dangerous to be caught asleep during the day; but although this being constantly on the alert and under supervision was irksome at the time, it actually proved a godsend as it kept us permanently employed. Besides we enjoyed seeing how little we could do without being bowled out.

Yosh remained an enigma. No one really understood him, and we used to wonder how this strangely complex human dynamo had evolved. We had never seen nor could we imagine him as a normal human being, outside his tyrannous role. Yet his nature was contradictory. He forced us to hate him but longed to be popular. He could beat a body to pulp, then provide comforts for a dying man. He was callous in the extreme, but at the same time respectful to the dead.

Religion scared him somewhat - he treated the Padre with some awe, thinking perhaps that Gerald could put a curse on him.

We knew Yosh was not married and he never spoke of his family, so it seemed that he had never had any home life. Perhaps it was a sense of insecurity that forced him to excesses beyond his control.

Whatever the truth was, he remained the object and centre of hate for everyone and as the tide of war turned we looked forward to the time when we could bring him to justice. For if there was one thing I was determined to do, it was to get even with this monster. If necessary I would go round the world to get him.

He knew that, obviously, but it did not curb him. In fact, the increasing certainty of retribution seemed only to inspire him to greater acts of malice.

6

"The Mews"

At the end of 1942, the officers were given a literary task. We were ordered by the Nips to write some essays on the war and what we thought of the Japanese fighting man. A tricky, even dangerous pastime; but we were not going to be trapped in this way. I gave the general directive, which was to write without giving offence, but at the same time to let there be no doubt what we thought of aggressive war.

We all wrote very much the same thing, and I censored all the essays. On the first subject we took the line that we as a peace-loving nation were always loth to fight a war which must bring misery both to victors and vanquished; but, once forced to take up arms in defence of what we considered a righteous cause, we would never lay them down until we achieved our aim. Though we had experienced certain setbacks and difficulties, we were absolutely confident of the ultimate victory of our armed forces. We rather enjoyed writing this, knowing it was bound to annoy the Nips without giving them reasonable cause for offence.

As for our opinion of the Japanese fighting man, we all just wrote a few guarded lines saying that we had only met a few whilst in captivity and that they appeared to understand their duty: faint enough praise with which to damn the lot of them. Obviously they wanted something they could use as propaganda. They knew of course they would get a lot of duds, but had hoped a few would suit their book. They were unlucky.

I am often asked why, in such conditions, they did not just make up an essay and declare that it was written by a P.O.W. Somehow that would not have been quite the same thing. The Japanese are curious people. Though naturally mendacious, they are scrupulous about having a grain of truth in their statements. This was noticeable throughout. Even Yosh required some justification, though often only the slightest, to start a scene.

I never discovered what the official reaction was to our essays, but I am certain that they were the primary cause of most of the officers being sent on the next draft. A party of two hundred was formed in the New Year. Just where they were to go no one knew, only we guessed it was in the tropics as tropical clothing and nets were provided.

All the fit officers were originally included in the draft. I believe they intended teaching us a lesson for our arrogant essays; besides Yosh would thus save about thirty hands for his outside working parties as we were not permitted to leave the camp in any circumstances whatsoever.

When the final medical inspection took place, a most cursory affair, I had passed the doctor and was about to join the party when the Camp Commandant - it was one of the rare occasions on which he attended - turned me back saying that I was Number One of the British and was not to go. He also turned back the Padre and Doctor Wyatt, whom he reckoned would be better employed at Macassar tending the sick and dying.

Nine other officers were unfit because of malaria and ulcers, while the remaining twenty-nine officers and 171 men formed the party. Yosh, I am sure, was a bit disappointed not to get rid of me.

They left on January 17th, 1943. I remember the day well as it was the twentieth anniversary of my joining the Navy, and two hours after their departure an Allied aircraft with four engines flew over the camp about 200 feet over the trees tops. It was a very exciting moment - that first sight of friends since our capture, and I recall how we envied the crew who would probably be back in their mess in Darwin, Australia in about three or four hours time.

With twenty-nine fewer officers our quarters became very comfortable and quiet - a pleasant change from what we had been used to. In the past nine months we had progressed considerably from our first billet in a large hut near the gate, where we had slept on the bare floor spread with "bedding" in the shape of torn up Dutch army paybooks found in large numbers in the barracks.

Hutted P.O.W. camp at Macassar

Now we lived in "The Mews" as we called our series of twelve rooms in a row, each about sixteen feet deep by eight wide, with a three-quarter partition dividing the front half from the rear. Normally we used the front for a sitting-room and the rear for sleeping. Yosh had said I was to have one room to myself, but I thought this was an unjustified advantage when all the rest were so crowded, so I shared mine with three officers in the next room. We used one for sleeping and dressing and the other partly as a sitting-room and partly as an office.

However, now that each of us could nearly have a room to himself, we were still forced to waste most of the accommodation because of the shortage of mosquito nets and mattresses. By joining two mattresses, four of us were able to sleep under one big mosquito net originally acquired by Lieutenant Commander F.R. Twiss, the *Exeter*'s Gunnery Officer, and known as the "four-in-hand". To this net I owe the fact that I never got malaria. I was one of the very few who escaped.

Despite Yosh, the next eight months were fairly reasonable in these quarters. They were at the far end of the camp away from the guard room and the gate, so we were not disturbed by the guards; nor were we in the vicinity of where Yosh was wont to cast loose, which was usually at the gate. Our men's barracks were within stones-throw, which was convenient for administration and control.

At one end of "The Mews" was a coconut grove with grass and shade, about thirty yards square. There I used to walk up and down every evening from five to six, generally with the Padre. I rarely missed my hour's walk per day throughout captivity and am certain it was responsible for the maintenance of my health - I was hardly ever ill throughout the three and a half years; certainly never at Macassar, although I did have some trouble from septic blisters on the feet.

The camp was three hundred yards square with roads along the perimeter and down the centre. The barrack blocks lay between the roads, and smaller buildings like "The Mews," offices, galleys, and hospital between the perimeter roads and the fence. In the vicinity of the barracks were large trees for shade - rain trees, I believe they were called, not very attractive but very shady. All open spaces were grass and we made flower gardens in front of the blocks. The whole place was rather like a park in which ugly barrack buildings had been placed. At one end was a large football field and at the other jungle, and at the rear a number of cottages which had been married quarters. The main coast road ran past the gate, but we could not see the sea, though sometimes we heard it as it was about three hundred yards beyond. There was no view of the outside world.

We spent most of our spare time reading. We played bridge and those who did not know the game were soon taught by those who did. We tried parlour games. One introduced by the Padre, involved collecting six people together and getting each to read something for about ten minutes. The diversity of their choice was fascinating, and two memorable passages I recall were: the Padre himself reading the Preface to the Authorised Version of the Bible, a *tour de force* of almost sublime sycophancy; and a Welsh officer reading from *How Green Was My Valley* with the enchanting lilt that only a Welshman could give it.

Looking back, there were times when life was almost pleasant in Macassar. I remember best the delightful tropical evenings as we sat outside "The Mews" on our homemade bamboo chairs discussing every topic under the sun, gossiping, yarning. Naturally too from time to time we fell out with each other. This was inevitable and in many ways quite a good thing: it was a safety-valve, and one usually felt better after a good blow-off.

We had of course our magnificent library of 1,200 books which we catalogued and kept in one of the quarters in "The Mews". There were books to suit every taste and among them several technical books which proved very useful. From one I learned the rudiments of astronomy, from another ship construction. I also studied French, but unfortunately my notes were confiscated, along with those of the other officers, just before we left for Java. The Japanese thought we had been keeping diaries and were loth to let us keep any records which might later be used as evidence against them.

Study was one of the main amenities available during the period we spent in captivity. Among the Dutch were people who could speak a wide assortment of modern languages, and without exception they welcomed the opportunity to impart their knowledge.

Some people carved things, mostly pipes. A pipe I still have was carved by one of our cooks with a broken table knife. It is a beautiful piece of work. Surprisingly, we were issued with tobacco which came to us packed in thick hollow bamboos. The ration was small, allowing for a consumption of about five cigarettes or two pipes per day. It was native tobacco and varied a lot in quality; generally, the blacker it was the better, while the pale stuff, resembling that found in a Virginia cigarette, was in fact pretty foul, besides burning your throat and palate. However it could be rendered milder by soaking in a solution of sugar and water and drying the fibres in the sun. A thickish paper was issued for rolling it in, but a number of people preferred to use a pipe.

There was a modicum of sport in the camp. The Dutch and ourselves played the odd football match in bare feet, and the Americans played baseball, and all three contingents boxed. Actually the Nips encouraged boxing. Oddly enough, the man who got the 207-stroke beating was our heavyweight. The "crime" he committed in no sense deserved the punishment he got, which suggests that Yosh made a particular point of trying to bring him down, but he failed.

We had religious services: indeed on occasions in the early days we were ordered to by the Nips: "All men play" (pray). Although these services were later stopped - Nips were suspicious of anything they could not understand - we were encouraged by Yosh to hold them clandestinely. He once caught my eye and made the sign of the cross followed by a drinking gesture, saying I was to meet him at the guardhouse after dark. When I got there he gave me a bottle of port for use as communion wine.

The Padre, by some strange and quite remarkable chance, had acquired an English prayer book, hymn book and Bible. The first two were found by a British working party sent to demolish one of the houses destroyed in the fighting in Macassar - they came across the books in a pile of rubbish. The Bible came from an Australian airman who was shot down in north Celebes and sent to our camp in April 1942. He was given the Bible by a native who rushed up and pressed it in his hand as he was being marched through the town.

Those books were invaluable to Gerald who, as the only minister of religion in the camp, was responsible for the spiritual welfare of us all. With them he buried people of many and varied denominations; between the Americans, Dutch and ourselves we numbered sixteen different Christian sects, added to which he composed funeral services for four Jews.

There was also one Moslem, but in this case Padre FitzGerald was not able to use any of his religious books; though, of course, not for any theological reasons. The incident occurred after I had left for Java, so I think you should have an account of it in his own words:

> One night I was roused in the early hours by a Nip, who indicated I was required to go to the gate. Being called out like that could only mean bad news.
>
> At the gate everything seemed quiet, which was surprising; but I soon discovered why. A Dutch doctor came up and pointed to a dark object on the ground, which he said was a coffin with, in it, an Indonesian. "They want you to read the burial service," he said.
>
> "But is the man a Christian?" I asked.
>
> "That's most unlikely."
>
> "Then his own people should bury him. I can't interfere."
>
> The doctor explained: "The Japanese insist that you do it. They put a live electric wire round their vegetable garden to stop the natives coming in, and this man has got killed. The sentries are going to bury him in the camp, to hush up the matter, but they are afraid his ghost will haunt them unless he's properly buried by a priest."
>
> At that point Yosh came up with a lantern and said in Malay, "Prayers, prayers."
>
> I hadn't thought of prayers, and had come without my prayer book, but was too scared of the man to admit such an omission, he being capable of beating up anybody, anytime, anywhere. So instinctively I put my hand to the pocket of my old Dutch service jacket, and there, bless me, was the book I was currently reading - Beaumarchais' *Le Barbier de Seville.* I think I held it upside down. That made no difference to the Nip, because I said the prayers I by then knew by heart, having read them often enough. And I asked the Almighty to forgive the deception, but He knew I was putting on this show to avoid a lot of trouble....

Viewed as a whole, life in the camp was utterly drab and monotonous. There had been a canteen native who came in with things like razor blades, toothpaste and pencils, but after a while Yosh banished him. Not one of the thousands of parcels sent by the Red Cross ever reached us in Macassar. We had no mail, in or out, no knowledge of our families. We did not even know if they were aware of our fate, which was a worry to all of us but especially to those who were married.

Life was devoid of practically everything which could have made it tolerable in our predicament - a reasonably satisfied stomach, elementary comfort in the way of a chair and bed of sorts, a change of clothes, decent footwear, an adequate supply of medicines, soap, shaving gear, music, art, the proper opportunities for religious worship and reliable war news - though the Dutch were believed to have a secret radio and fed us occasionally with the important items of news.

We were each allowed one wireless message in November 1942 - ten words, some of which were compulsory. These messages were broadcast, a few at a time, over a long period. Mine was in fact intercepted by an amateur in February 1943. My people had no news after that until my first letter from Java, which they did not get until 1945, eighteen months after I had written it.

The working parties went out at 8 a.m., when work began for the camp, and they worked, except for an hour off for lunch, until 5 p.m. They got Sunday off. The only other day of rest I recall was Christmas Day, 1942, when Yosh ordered us to "enjoy" ourselves, and decided that the best way we could do it was by having a concert.

The concert, as you can imagine turned out to be a complete flop. Next day when the Padre and I discussed the reason for this, as we paced the coconut grove, he quoted the 137th Psalm:

> By the waters of Babylon we sat down and wept: when we remembered thee, O Sion.
>
> As for our harps, we hanged them up: upon the trees that are therein.
>
> For they that led us away captive required of us then a song, and melody, in our heaviness: Sing us one of the songs of Sion.

How shall we sing the Lord's song: in a strange land?

One of our innocent diversions was making secret fun of our Japanese guards. It was a tricky, sometimes dangerous pastime, but that only added spice to it. Perhaps it may sound a bit elemental as humour, getting ignorant foreigners to say ridiculous things in your language, yet to have any sort of a laugh on our bullying guards gave us a certain feeling of satisfaction.

They used to ask what was meant by "You .... little yellow bastard," and we used to reply, much to the Australians' annoyance, that it meant they were bosom friends of the Australians.

One young Nip called Modi was very keen to pick up a few phrases in English. One day he asked how he should address a British officer, and some wags, having explained that the English translation of his name was mud, told him that the way to do it was to stand to attention, salute and say, "Good morning, sir. My name is mud, sir. It looks like rain today." Modi learnt this, and whenever he saw any of us, he would go through the performance. With a tropical sun in a blue sky it sounded even funnier than it was; and we would laugh and give him a clap and a "Bagoos" (Malay for good) which always delighted him.

There was one guard whom we all liked, the only Japanese I ever met whose character suggested that they might have the gentle virtues. His name was Ini and, I believe, in civilian life he had been a Shintoist priest. True or not, I do know that he never took part in the beat-ups, and indeed tried wherever possible to smooth things over. Moreover, while the other guards were kept very much on their toes by Yoshida - they frequently appeared with black eyes and bruised faces from the beatings-up they too received - Ini seemed to be able to get away with anything.

He would often come down to "The Mews" and talk to us for most of the time he was supposed to be patrolling the camp, and sometimes he would even put his rifle under the table, take off his puttees and boots, and put his feet up. One evening he had been talking to us, when we suddenly realised it was nearly ten o'clock - time for him to go off duty and for us to go to bed. We pointed this out to him, so he put on his boots, stuffed his puttees into his pocket and went off. Then the bugle sounded and we turned in.

A short while later we heard the crump of boots on the road and knew it must be a Japanese, as everyone else wore clogs. On this a few people put up a few convincing snores. The Nip went into the Padre's room and a few moments later emerged roaring with laughter. It was Ini and as soon as he was able he explained the joke. He had gone to the guardhouse, saluted the sergeant and reported all was well, at which point he was asked what had happened to his rifle as he did not have it with him. His reply apparently was that he did not know, but would go and look for it. And, ah, there it was under the table!

The very fact of a Nip guard being able to get away with such a thing is so incredible that there must have been something very special about Ini. Any other guard would have been severely punished, to say nothing of the repercussions that might have been visited upon us, under whose table the rifle had been "concealed".

Later, when things got pretty bad in this camp, Ini was put in charge of the bicycle party, a group of about a dozen men whose job it was to repair the Nips' bicycles. The bicycle party was one of those on which the sick could always be sent when things got too hot for them in hospital. The party would be marched to the bicycle shop in the town, where Ini not only allowed them to take things easy but he actually spent his own money buying them food and cigarettes.

So fond were the men of Ini that after liberation their first thought was for him. A P.O. went to the Padre to see if he could have some of the American cigarettes which had been issued to the contingent.

"By all means," said the Padre, "but who are they for?"

"Oh, for Ini. We heard he likes Yank cigarettes, and felt we would like him to be well looked after."

When it rained in Macassar it certainly rained. It could bucket down at the rate of ten inches a day, sometimes for ten days at a stretch. The wet season lasted three months, with odd spells of fine weather breaking the monotony of the rain, and the steamy hot-house atmosphere in the huts. Towards the end of the monsoon, late in

February, the fine days came more frequently and the rainy periods got shorter; till one day in March there would be a fine morning like any other except that the smoke from the galley chimney was blowing the other way. The wind had changed, and probably until the following December there would be no rain at all. Now it became hot but not too humid, on the whole a good climate for the tropics.

Contrary to our expectations, nobody got sunstroke, even after we lost our hair; some men in working parties used to work without hats in the scorching sun from eight in the morning to near six in the evening. The current medical theory is that sunstroke (heat exhaustion) is caused more through people being overdressed and over-fed while exposed to intense direct heat of the sun. As our men were practically naked, besides being in a state of semi-starvation, they were not affected.

We were actually five degrees south of the Equator; which meant that the length of the days varied by about ten minutes between mid-winter and mid-summer. There was little or no twilight. Sunset was about six, and a few minutes later it was black night. You get in Macassar what they call the Australian winter - a week in mid-June when the nights get cold, or rather cooler than the others. On those nights a blanket was adequate. Otherwise we slept with no bedclothes on.

The moment it got dark the mosquitoes came out, and for the first months of our captivity they made our nights a misery. Malaria spread rapidly, and at last the Nips decided we all had to have mosquito-nets. Yosh organised work parties for their manufacture, and soon practically the entire camp sweltered under low, canopied shrouds of thick calico with just a narrow strip of actual mosquito netting on top to let in some air. Fortunately for my bed-fellows and me, the Gunnery Officer's "four-in-hand" was the real thing, high vaulted and netted all round.

Because of the mosquitoes, those in hospital had to have their nets up the moment night fell. Since there were no lights in the wards, this was in effect like putting a hood over a birdcage, consigning the sick man for twelve interminable and stifling hours of darkness.

Most of the rest of the camp had a certain amount of very dim electric lighting, though it was very difficult to get the Nips to replace dud bulbs. A black-out was supposed to be in force, but it was never very rigidly enforced.

In their anti-malaria measures, the Japanese were of course quite right, but, as in most other things they attempted, here too they went to ridiculous limits. They had heard of the great mosquito-destruction campaigns carried out in other parts of the world, and determined to repeat the success in our camp. But instead of using insecticides, prisoners were at times put on mosquito-hunting duties.

Each had a card or paper which had to be neatly ruled into fifty squares, and when the sentries went round at night he had to produce his card with a dead mosquito in each square.

At first the task seemed formidable - going round every day and catching or swatting fifty mosquitoes. Then somebody came up with a bright idea. A string was tied to an empty tin, the sides of which were coated with grease. This was then swung about in the water-logged air-raid shelters, and in next to no time the grease would be clogged black with trapped mosquitoes.

In the beginning we cooked some of our own food, which we had bought at the canteen. But Yosh soon put a stop to that. After a while we were all issued with a plate and knife, fork and spoon, and we each acquired a tin to hold our rice. At meal times our food would be brought to us from the galley.

After the initial period in which we were deliberately starved to reduce us to a state of submissiveness, our rations were slightly increased. We each got every day roughly about 12oz. dry bread, 6oz. rice with a little coarse meat, greens and/or a duck egg and half a cup of thin coffee. In 1943 the bread was stopped altogether, and instead we got more rice and also half an ounce of sugar. On occasions, we were given fish or an egg in place of meat, while the type and quantities of vegetables varied a good deal. Later meat, fish and eggs disappeared entirely, after which we existed on a diet composed mainly of rice and greens, in weight between 1½ and 2lb. per day.

The lack of vitamins and protein in the diet led to widespread deficiency diseases. To supplement our ration we grew some papayas, as well as local spinach, tomatoes and sweet potatoes, but it was never very much as our allotment was not big enough. With a little organis-ation and at no extra cost to themselves the Japanese could have vastly increased our rations. Given the space we could have produced all our own fruit and vegetables, but they obstinately turned a deaf ear to all our representations. Even at first when no salt was provided and we suggested that if our cook could add a bucket of water from the sea, three hundred yards away, it would make all the difference, they refused to allow it.

We often wondered whether our abortive efforts at sea to stem the Japanese advance towards Australia had done any good at all. All the Allied heavy units and many other smaller ships and auxiliaries had been lost. The British "D" class cruisers had been withdrawn just in time and the Australian cruiser *Hobart* had escaped, but otherwise it was one disaster after another. It appeared to us that we had achieved very little and at great sacrifice. The enemy had captured the whole of Malaya and the Dutch West Indies and the way was open to Australia. We felt at times that we had been needlessly thrown away.

On later, and more reasoned, reflection a very different picture emerged. It came to our knowledge that the Japanese Navy had guaranteed to transport their military and air forces direct to Australia, by-passing Malaya and the West Indies, but that their army had not been prepared to accept this strategy. The army demanded they should first neutralise the flank of their lines of communication. No doubt behind the latter alternative lay the thought of the rich prizes in South-east Asia ready for plucking, apart from the prestige value of the capture of Singapore. The Japanese High Command had reckoned that if they destroyed the American Fleet in a surprise attack on Pearl Harbour, it would take the Americans eighteen months to recover. During this period, they would consolidate what they called the "Iron

Ring," stretching in a great arc from Burma through to Midway, and invade Australia.

The potential threat of our naval forces to their flank in a direct assault on Australia had forced their army into the East Indian Archipelago, and they must have lost many thousands of men in the process. Having got them in by March 1942, they then had to get them out for their further advance to the south-east and this took several months.

But the Americans recovered from Pearl Harbour, not in eighteen months, but in six months, and they mustered sufficient strength to ward off the enemy advance, first at the battle of the Coral Sea in May, and in the next month at Midway. The battle of Midway, with the destruction of the main might of the Japanese aircraft carrier strength, proved one of the most decisive battles in world history. The Japanese advance was held at Rabaul and Guadacanal and the invasion of Australia never took place.

Thus, our naval operations had produced a strategic victory and our sacrifice had helped to save Australia.

From January to August 1943 conditions at Macassar were better than at any time. The camp organisation improved, and men had become acclimatised and accustomed to captivity. Discipline was back to form and morale extraordinarily high. The success of the North Africa landing and then the invasion of Italy were great news, and the American advance across the Pacific was followed with keen interest.

We were all naturally confident of victory, but what I think really sustained us was an unquenchable optimism about the date of our release. At no time can I remember any sailor believing we would still be in Macassar much more than six months ahead. "Out by Christmas" lasted from May to December, then "Out by Easter" from January to April. "It won't be long now" was the catch-phrase of the super-optimistic; and some of them used it whenever they greeted you. They were suspected of sleeping in their clogs to make sure they were not adrift when the final "*yasume*" was sounded; "*yasume*" being

Japanese for rest or stand easy, and one of the first enemy words we learnt from our guards.

Meanwhile Yosh had steadily taken over complete control of the camp; now nothing was done without his permission. The only guard who was not completely dominated by his overpowering personality was Ueno, a rather high-class Nip in charge of the galley. As a result he did not stay long; he was sent up to Maros. Yosh had got rid of him as he did a succession of guard commanders, who on the whole were not too bad, beyond their innate sadistic proclivity and an inability to control him.

Hatayama was the first, then Mori, then Shimahama. Then came Okubo and Notomi, both very weak with Yosh and rather double-faced through fear of him. Okubo died in captivity awaiting trial; and Notomi was later condemned to death and executed. I rather liked him and personally never had any trouble with him; though I gather he later turned nasty as the war worsened for them, and became in fact an agent provocateur for Yosh.

In April 1943 after the wet season, I was involved in a really big scene with Yosh. We had a lot of sickness, especially malaria cases and mostly from Maros. H.Q. had obviously complained to Yosh about the lack of man-power for work and he decided to rectify this.

A meeting was convened in the Dutch Colonel's house, which all S.O.s of units were to attend together with their medical representatives. To summon us came the interpreter. He was a Dutch officer who, unfortunately, was not very good at Japanese and often translated incorrectly. I was sorry for him, as he tried hard and he had a very difficult time. Yosh hated him, so the poor man got beaten up just because he was present during a scene.

That day he came over to our quarters during the dinner hour and said, "Mistair Cooper, Yoshida wants you and the Doctor in the Colonel's house now. He is going to beat you both up for having so many sick in the hospital." Which was not exactly a jolly way of breaking the news to us.

However, we went over to the meeting place, there to find Yosh sitting at the table with his back to us, making a lot of noise. The

Dutch adjutant was at the other end of the table - impassive, quiet, calm, and dignified. The senior Dutch doctor was sitting on one side of the table; Yosh liked and admired him and he was always safe. The American S.O., a squat little lieutenant-commander, was opposite the doctor - silent, subdued and obviously worried. Shimahama, to our surprise, was there too; he was rarely present in a scene but obviously was in trouble with H.Q. as well.

Doc Wyatt took off his spectacles before we entered; he was not going to have them broken by Yosh's fist, or risk the damage of broken glass in his face. Yosh did not see us enter; and, knowing he was as likely as not to go for the person he sent for immediately on seeing him, rather like a dog on suddenly seeing a cat, we went straight to the other side of the table. It was an elementary precaution, getting it between him and us.

The conference, or Yosh's tirade, continued for sometime. His main complaint was that there were too many men in hospital, and too many English at that; all of which had, piecemeal, to be interpreted. Then the interpreter made some mistake which aggravated Yosh, who struck him several times in the face. The Dutchman wore a pince-nez; and to protect it put his hand up and took it off. Any movement like that always infuriated the Nips, as they suspected you were about to strike them back; and for it he got several more in the face. On top of that he tried to argue in Japanese which only made things worse. Yosh got more and more out of control, and, finally banishing the interpreter to the roadway outside to stand to attention, thundered at me that all the British in hospital, one hundred and sixty-one, were to be discharged to their barracks forthwith.

"All right," I replied, to quieten him, knowing that he would not enforce this.

The interpreter was then called back to interpret something to do with the Dutch. But again something went wrong, and Yosh suddenly went quite mad. Getting up, he rushed outside, found a pick-axe and brought it back into the room. He raised it as if to strike and I thought he was going to kill the interpreter. Instead he crashed it down on the floor and knocked off the iron head. Then, armed with the handle, he started banging the table.

Luckily, the nearest were the Dutch doctor and Shimahama whom he would never have touched. He gave the interpreter a few for good measure, then started dictating directives in Japanese for translation, emphasising each point with a crash of the pick-handle on the table, and working himself up to let loose on any of us at any moment.

I was wearing a white tropical shirt, and looking down I could see my heart beating through the material. The pocket on my left breast was just heaving in and out. It shook me as I realised I must be in a state to get like this. I thought I must be cracking up. Afterwards, when I mentioned it to the Doc, and asked whether that was to be expected or whether it was abnormal, he said it was both. He pointed out that such a reaction was inevitable in an emotional scene of that intensity and that it was no doubt accentuated by the fact we were anaemic through lack of protein.

Fortunately for us, just when Yosh was about to lose complete control, Shimahama considered it was about time the scene ended, and end it he did. Actually I think they had trumped up most of it to terrorise us into discouraging sickness at all costs.

Shimahama, speaking quiet Japanese, said he realised that the men at Maros had been defeated by malaria, but that they must now try to conquer it: how they were to do that he did not explain for, once caught, malaria was impossible to shake off without regular and adequate quinine, and that was not forthcoming from the Nips.

Anyhow the scene gradually quietened down. Yosh gave a few ridiculous orders and we were told to "hoosh", which I think was slang for "arimas" which meant "done", "finished", "all correct". That evening the hospital list was reduced by three British, one American and one Dutch. So much for Yoshida's threats.

There were times, in my effort to avoid trouble, that I had to sail pretty close-hauled to the wind of Nip policy. Unpleasant decisions were necessary in order to protect the whole community, and some of our men were at times inclined to think I was "Nip happy". They did not see the whole picture. My main responsibility was to the sick who were always the first and most vulnerable target for Yosh.

There were times when I thought I was starting to crack up: living on one's nerves is not to be recommended for a prisoner-of-war in the hands of the Japanese. I prayed for deliverance from the malice and machinations of the monster who starved us, baited us, tortured us, and above all used us to quench the libido of his hate and cruelty.

Further I prayed to be preserved from his immoderate efficiency. If anything took away from his truly outstanding qualities as a leader it was his fanaticism about having everything just so. His sense of exactitude would never leave him alone. Anything out of place tormented him. He was meticulously tidy. Moreover, he was of a frugal nature, and the sight of anything being wasted would detonate in his brain a chain reaction of explosive violence. At least this was predictable, and we could and did take steps to prevent the detonating flash; yet the sheer malignancy of the man sought ways and means of deliberately setting it off.

An example of this occurred on June 15th, 1943. Yosh had started night rounds very much on our own naval lines. The executive officer of each contingent had to muster at the gate at 8.45, then proceed to his own area. David Chubb acted as our executive officer; he got on much better with Yosh than I did; actually he handled him rather well, and Yosh liked him. From the commencement of rounds everyone in the camp was meant to stand silent and still until they were over, though of course no one did until Yosh was within sight and hearing. Barracks had to be spotless and tidy; which naturally gave him plenty of scope any time he wanted trouble.

Often he exercised fire stations afterwards. In this evolution each barrack had to produce two buckets of water and one of sand, besides spades and other implements; the fire party had to proceed at full speed, running on clogs through the pitch black camp, and Heaven help any man who faltered or spilt a drop of water on the way. Yosh had a bee in his bonnet about conserving water, and as for his finding a tap left on - well, that could always be counted on to detonate one of those mental explosions I have mentioned.

That June evening I sensed trouble in the air before rounds started, and soon after we heard him making a lot of noise in the Dutch barracks. Having gone through these, he crossed the no-man's-land between them and the British barracks, then suddenly turned off his track and went into our bathroom. And there, to David's astonishment and dismay, a tap was running full on, the water already overflowing from a large concrete bath.

How the tap came to be on is a mystery. That it was off only a few minutes before, we were quite certain, and it was our belief that someone had been told by Yosh to turn it on. Yosh always needed a mote of justification.

The scene that ensued can be numbered among the major ones, with Yosh at his loudest and blood-curdling worst. I heard him from "The Mews," and thought, and hoped, he was having a go at the Dutch. But before long I distinguished the familiar cry of "*Ku-pa! Ku-pa!*" Then the Dutch bugler boy arrived. His job was to precede the rounds party blowing the alert. He said that Yosh wanted me in No. 28 barrack.

I walked across the road, through No. 29, into the big hall known as No. 25. Yosh was there beating up the coxswain of the *Stronghold.* As I entered he swung round and gave me four straight rights under the chin. I managed to stay upright but did not know exactly what was happening, beyond the sparks in front of my eyes.

Yosh then turned again to the coxswain, and I was able to ask David in a whisper what the trouble was. He murmured, "Tap running". Then I saw that he too had been beaten up; in fact he had been the first to cop it, before Yosh had stormed into No. 28, punched a chief petty officer on the jaw and knocked him flying, and then started on the coxswain.

From No. 25 he went into No. 29, where he let fly with his boot in the crutch of a stoker P.O. who fortunately was too quick for him and stepped back. The blow missed, but the P.O. fell against the table and one of his clogs came off. Yosh was on it like a flash, picking it up and crashing it down on the P.O.s head. Then he threw down the clog and stormed on through the block like a demented whirlwind shouting, "*Api! Api! Api!*"

"*Api*" is Malay for "fire," and away went the fire parties at full speed. I thought it was a good time to retire from the scene, as I was not a specified attendant at fire drill, and knowing from bitter experience that my presence only aggravated a situation. I went into my quarters and there, from a short distance, watched anxiously. But not for long. Again "*Ku-pa!*" So out again to be met on arrival with another salvo on the chin.

I suppose there were about a hundred men in the fire party, all fallen in with their buckets and spades and as motionless as statues. Glaring at them, Yosh started all over again about the waste of water, taps left running, and big trouble always with the bad English contingent. It was a fantastic tirade, a bravura of vituperation in slang Japanese and Malay punctuated throughout by his favourite abusive epithet - "*karexema*". A lot of "*karexemas*" was always bad news. The word was our barometer.

The Americans were also a target that night - they used the same bathroom and were therefore implicated. Their executive officer was sent for and arrived in the arena; by which time Yosh had grabbed a long-handled spade, so welcomed him with six of the best. Then David got a second helping, and my turn naturally followed. For my first five he used the back of the spade, but with the last one I heard a swish as he turned it to catch me across the buttocks with the edge. That one did me no good at all.

Yosh then fell out the Dutch and ordered the British and Americans to remain fallen in till dawn. But the "Magnesium Flame" was beginning to subside, and we were soon to see him retire to the guardhouse. Half an hour later, a fat, genial Nip nicknamed Formosa sauntered up and started talking in Malay. Someone translated. He said that Yosh was now out of the camp and he, as sergeant of the guard, had full powers. He promised he would send us to bed in ten minutes time, and he added that such scenes would continue to occur until someone else wore the yellow armband.

At 10.30 he fell us out and we retired, sore and worn out to our beds. There was a nightmarish quality about the whole set up. It seemed we were inside a lunatic asylum, but one in which the lunatics were those in charge. Have no doubt about it, the thought was very real; we had already noticed that the moon had a very definite effect on Yoshida.

"*Yoshida tidah bagoos*" (Yoshida no good) Formosa had said. It was the understatement of all time.

7

The Pomalaa Party

It took some time before we discovered where our two hundred comrades had been sent. It was to a little hell on the west side of the eastern leg of Celebes called Pomalaa. The Dutch who knew this place shook their heads. There was precious little in Pomalaa besides a nickel mine and malaria, which was not a good look out for our party, ill-clothed, unshod, without medicines and practically starving.

We were worried at first, but when we could do nothing about it we put it out of our minds. Bad news, sickness, death, beatings, hunger, misery and squalor were so commonplace that we had become callous and case-hardened to them. Personally, I think I am still a bit like that; I saw so many cases of malaria in which anyone with a temperature of less than 104 degrees was not considered worth worrying about, that it is still difficult for me to be impressed by anything less.

In July, there were certain indications that the Pomalaa party were expected back - we had to clear part of the barracks for them in anticipation of their return. Then everything went quiet for about six weeks, and we began to think of something else that had been on the cards for some time - the despatch overseas of the officers.

I viewed any move with mixed feelings; in fact I hated the idea of leaving the men. Morale and discipline were pretty good, and with David squaring Yosh the dual control worked well. I was quite certain too that my presence was beneficial to them. Although Yosh hated me and went out of his way to humiliate me, he never quite forgot that I was a lieutenant-commander of some standing while he was only a 3rd class P.O., to which rate he had just been promoted. The thought undoubtedly curbed him and restrained him in his excesses.

I certainly did not relish the thought of being drafted overseas. The most likely places to which we might be sent were Japan, Singapore and Java, in that order. I had no wish to see the great

Nippon, nor did I want to be hungry and cold; being hungry and hot was bad enough but preferable, despite the greater chances of disease. Singapore was known to be vile as it was run by the Japanese Army. Yosh used to threaten us with drafting to a Japanese Army camp as a punishment and he made it sound even worse than his own. Java seemed the least of the three evils, though with Allied submarines and aircraft now patrolling East Indian waters the chances of surviving any sea voyage were poor. Moreover, we all thought that the East Indies offered us hopes of a better and earlier release than either Malaya or Nippon.

There was however one main advantage in a move, and that was getting away from Yoshida, and from time to time it seemed the only one that mattered.

The Pomalaa party returned in the middle of September 1943. Two days before their arrival we were told that only one hundred and eighty-four were coming back. That meant sixteen deaths, or 8 per cent, in eight months. We did not go much on this and showed it, so Yoshida explained that all had died of disease and not through working for the Japanese. Doubtless there was a grain of truth in what he said - that disease had in fact killed them. But we were not credulous enough to swallow more than that grain.

Yosh also explained that many of the party were ill and all were dirty, which we accepted as a typical understatement and prepared for the worst. They were to be isolated on arrival, no contact of any sort being permitted under pain of all sorts of frightful punishments if anyone was caught breaking the rule. New arrivals were always isolated in this manner. Officially, it was for medical quarantine reasons, though actually the real one was to prevent any news in the possession of the incomers being passed on to the camp until a delay had been applied to it.

In preparing for the Pomalaa party Yosh was at his energetic best. Every spare bed to be found was rigged, old doors and wood planks were raked up to act as bed boards, open fires were built to boil water in large oil drums for disinfecting of clothes, hoses from fire hydrants were rigged to supply water. He was in good form, tireless and obviously keen to give the travellers the best welcome possible. I think he felt it a reflection on his country that some of *his* prisoners should have been treated in such a fashion, and he was going to rectify it. Some "face" had been lost.

Twice their day of arrival was postponed. Then on September 16th they arrived. They were due at 4 p.m. but the Nips were never very certain about times. I wandered down to the gate at 3.30 in case they should come early; I thought it important that they should be met by someone and shown that we had their welfare at heart. Ill and starving men are usually depressed, apathetic and looking for sympathy and care.

I had only been at the gate two minutes when the first lorry drove into camp. There was a lot of baggage in the back and a number of men on top. They were wearing round-brimmed straw hats very much like those which children wear in summer. The men were unshaven, rather grey in complexion and haggard. It was difficult to recognise them individually.

Someone was sitting next to the driver, waving his hand at me and smiling. He obviously knew me, but I could not at once place him. Then I suddenly realised it was the Sub - as Forecastle Officer he had always been with me when working cables, so it gave me a nasty shock to see him thus, almost impossible to recognise. Stunned, I just stood with rather a blank expression on my face as the lorries passed.

I took care not to call out or wave or sign with my hands. Yosh had made himself quite clear about our not attempting to contact the new arrivals under any circumstances. I was not going to have a row that day. He must be kept quiet at all costs. But by pressing my lips tightly together, I was able to indicate the need for silence, which I hoped would suggest the reason for my undemonstrative welcome. Their clothes were reddish with stain and so too were their skins. It was as if they had all been dipped in sheep dye. I learned later it was from the nickel ore on which they had been sitting for several days in the hold of a ship.

The moment they got off the lorries the machinery for their reception which Yosh had organised was set in motion. They were made to undress and put all their clothes in the drums for boiling. Then they went under a hose to wash themselves, and next were given a suit of camp-made linen shorts and singlet. David Chubb and I were detailed by Yosh to clean out the baths, a job we tackled gladly as we were pleased with what was being done. It was definitely Yosh's finest hour. He was in a very good temper and appeared sincerely sympathetic towards the party on account of their low standard of health. I remember his telling me they were very ill and in serious need of food and rest, which they would get now that they were back in his camp and under his command again. Not to worry. He would soon get them well. In a month's time, they would be working again.

This was one of the few occasions on which I ever had a personal and peaceful talk with Yoshida. He spoke Malay making allowance for my very elementary knowledge of the language, but I could easily understand him as he used words we had all learned to recognise - "*tidor*" (sleep), "*kerdja*" (work), "*makan*" (food), "*sakit*" (sick). He said that they would do no work, but were to take plenty of sun and light P.T. He would give them extra food. He did too, but was mean enough to take it out of rations that should have gone to the rest of the camp!

A bath and clean clothes, with a supper of boiled rice with a fried egg each and coffee put new heart into the Pomalaa party. The camp at this time was looking lovely. It was like a park, trim and well-kept, a veritable paradise to these men who had been in the jungle for eight months.

There were many hospital cases, besides a large number of others who were very ill. You could see the expressions of intense relief on their faces on arriving safely in this camp. I am told that even Yoshida on the jetty had come as a homely and reassuring sight. They believed they had been snatched from the jaws of death; for another three weeks in Pomalaa would probably have resulted in at least thirty more deaths. The ship which brought them had not been sunk, and at last they were reasonably safe. They were clean again for the first time in months, and they were with friends.

The Japanese too were being kind, so that they could at last just sit and rest, do nothing, recuperate. The fear of death had receded, at least for the time being. Many of them were unfortunately to die through the malice and neglect of our enemy, but that was not to be for yet another eighteen months.

Later I was to get a more detailed picture of what the Pomalaa people had been through. To begin with nearly the whole party of two hundred (twenty-nine officers, including two doctors, and one hundred and seventy-one men) had malaria when they started out, and about fifty had running sores, ulcers and septic wounds.

Their camp was about a mile south of Pomalaa and situated on the edge of the jungle in a mosquito-infested swamp area. The accommodation consisted of rough bamboo huts thatched with palm leaves. Bed boards, secured to a raised bamboo frame, gave each man a sleeping space of two and a half feet wide. Sanitary and hygiene arrangements were primitive and insufficient. Moreover the camp was rat infested.

They lived on a daily ration of 1 1/3lb. rice, with 2oz. poor quality vegetables, 2oz. sugar and some coffee. Occasionally they were given a little fresh or salt fish, and at times a salt egg. After strong protests, a small quantity of buffalo meat was also provided.

They had to do coolie work reclaiming a salt marsh - digging in slime and mud from 7 a.m. to 5 p.m. with two hours off for their midday meal. Naval guards from Kendari were responsible for discipline and working parties, and local Japanese civilians for food, welfare, medical supplies and direction of work. These civilians had shown a completely callous disregard for the welfare of the prisoners.

Shortly after their arrival at Pomalaa, there had been a serious resurgence of malaria followed by dysentery. Medicines were ridiculously inadequate especially quinine. Papaya leaves which are chewed by the natives as a quinine substitute were sometimes provided in lieu, but these too were frequently refused. Some men had thirty bouts of malaria in the eight months they were away and often with no quinine given to them at all. Within two months the protein and vitamin deficiency diseases had started, and men went down with beri-beri, pellagra, blindness, ulcers, scabies and septic bed sores. A list of their other ills included gastric troubles, heat exhaustion, dengue, prickly heat and general debility. No quinine at all from July 27th to August 31st resulted in eight deaths. By the end of August only nineteen men were fit for work, and even the Nips decided that it was better to call it a day and send them all back to Macassar.

Of the one hundred and eighty-four survivors who returned, only twenty-eight were able to walk more than a short distance. Sixty-eight were incapable of walking at all and had to be supported, and sixteen were dangerously ill.

Yosh's "no contact" orders were broken very quickly without anyone being caught. We signalled to each other by semaphore through the doorways across to the opposite windows. We sent notes hidden in rice, and after nightfall we made direct contact. We soon had all their news and they had ours. They had been without war news for eight months so we were able to tell them of the invasion of Italy and its collapse, the progress of the campaign against the U-boats in the Atlantic then at the height of its success, and various other items which were a shot in the arm for these sick men, some of whom were expected to die.

Another officer I could not recognise was Mark Kerr. He was a skeleton with beri-beri, malaria and dysentery. A few nights before, he had "died" for some minutes during a bad bout of malaria but had been resuscitated by one of the doctors. Medically speaking his survival was inexplicable, and that he continued to live was due entirely to his own indomitable courage. Most other men in a similar condition would have given up - collapsed and died in a few minutes. A man does not last long once he loses his mental stimulus, his will to live. But Mark just refused to die.

Later, we got used to drafts coming back from Pacific islands in such a state that individuals' best friends could not recognise them; which may explain why the return of our own men from Pomalaa might appear to have been recorded without appropriate feeling for the way in which comrades had been misused. We were shocked of course to see the way they had been reduced through disease and suffering, and "reduced" is scarcely the word. An officer named Southworth, once a first class scrum half as tough as they go, now weighed 6 stone 8 lb., the weight I had been at my prep school at the age of twelve. There were many others under 7 stone.

That was Pomalaa, another example of the malice that under-lay our ordeal at the hands of the Japanese.

8

Fair Winds for Java

It was October 2nd and we were definitely leaving. All the officers in the camp except those specially picked to remain by Yoshida were forming a draft of twenty-eight British, six Americans and 166 Dutch. Our destination was unknown, which was not a particularly nice feeling. The zero hour was 7.30 a.m.

We rose at 5.30 and had breakfast, then packed our belongings; all of mine went in one small pack. I then went round and said good-bye to the men in the barracks. We had not known definitely of our departure till after dark the night before, so I had not had a chance to see them, though I had written out a farewell message and given it to David Chubb to read after our departure. David, the Padre and a midshipman were the only British officers selected to remain, though there were also the warrant officers, whom the Nips claimed as ratings.

It was sad leaving the men, who were all great friends of mine by now, greater than I can explain. Prison life had bound us together with great ties of comradeship. But they seemed quiet and not particularly moved by our departure, and I thought it strange.

After being searched and deprived, as I have mentioned before, of our notebooks, we were fallen in and marched down to the gate. Small groups of men confined to barracks and the Pomalaa men waved us off.

About 250 of our men in working parties were fallen in at the gate. As we marched through them and out of the gate we gave them a chuck-up - wave, good luck and cheerio. They barely responded, standing there mute and nearly motionless. A few answered back, but only a few. What was wrong with them? Were they glad to get rid of us? I was staggered.

As we marched down the road I remarked about what had happened to my neighbours. John Hickley, who was No. 1 of

Encounter, turned to me and said, "Don't you understand? They didn't give us a send-off because they are speechless with disappointment, fed to the teeth. The idea of their officers leaving them has shaken them to the core. They feel alone and unprotected."

"Yes, you're probably right," I said. They had come to realise what a buffer the officers were between them and the Nips, and now obviously they viewed the future with alarm.

I considered the number of our officers left behind to be quite inadequate. The Padre, though a tower of strength and wisdom, was by reason of his calling non-executive. Most of the warrant officers were inexperienced at taking charge of large groups of men, besides not having the required status for the job, and the midshipman was very young. The whole weight devolved on David Chubb, a religious and sensitive person, with a taste for music, art and literature, more so perhaps than the average officer. Because of that, he suffered more than most from the grim realities of life in the camp, though of course he would be the last to show it. He was quite obviously going to have a very sticky time, and no one would have been in his shoes for love or money.

The march to the jetty was a fine experience. I had not been out of the camp for nineteen months, except on the back of lorries taking the dead to the cemetery, and on one occasion to the dentist. It was good to be striding down the road, to be able to see the sea, to look at the general life of the people, to see houses, gardens, flowers. It was good to be free of our prison camp. Good to be getting away from Yosh. It was a different walk from the one when we arrived in Macassar. Now any change was exciting and exhilarating.

We halted on the jetty alongside a medium-sized cargo liner called the *Rio de Janeiro Maru*. She looked clean and habitable. But before we embarked they had to count us again and by their lists we were one short. Only twenty-eight British instead of twenty-nine. I pointed out that Rae, one of the midshipmen from Pomalaa, was too ill to travel and that his name had been erased; the doctors had assured me they had told Yoshida and all was in order.

Yosh was very angry. He jumped on his motor cycle combination and was away back to camp. The midshipman, who was barely seventeen when we were taken prisoner, had had malaria continuously for nearly eight months. He was little more than a skeleton, anaemic to a degree and really ill. Yet he was grabbed off his sick-bed by Yosh, beaten up, then thrown into the sidecar while his friends chucked in his few belongings with him, and driven down to the harbour.

Meanwhile we had embarked and had been piled into the after hold, all 200 of us. The naval officer in charge of the draft was not a bad fellow and quite approachable. Being a sailor, he was quite interested to speak to me and I was able to make some requests to him. I explained that the missing officer was quite unfit to travel in a hold of a ship and in that atmosphere. I pointed out that I doubted if he would survive the voyage; as it was, he was only just alive.

Soon the midshipman arrived. He could just stand but the journey to the docks and the scene with Yosh had taken a lot out of him. He had fever and was almost in a collapsed state. Our doctor did not like his pulse or breathing. We got the Nip naval officer over to see him and showed him how unwise it was. He just said, "All right, send him back." Yosh looked daggers. John Hickley and I took him up on deck and on to the jetty. He could not walk without his arms round our necks; we half carried him to a lorry and put him in the seat alongside the driver. He kept saying, "After all this trouble, don't send me back. I'd rather come with you." But I told him, "No. No. Much better you go back. You'll be far better off in the camp. You'll get well there."

"But Yoshida will probably start on me again."

"No he won't," I said. "He has had his go and with him, once a scene is over, it's over."

We said good-bye to him and wandered back to the gangway. There we met Shimahama, Okubo, Notomi. All three shook hands with me, wished me good-bye and good luck, and saluted me. Yosh was there too, talking to the new Camp Commandant, a brute of a fellow in the Kempetai. While I was still at the gangway, the Commandant got in the sidecar and Yosh got on the pillion behind another Nip.

Yosh looked at me and smiled faintly, nothing more. I looked right through him with as much distaste and hate as I could put into my stare. I wanted him to know how glad I was to see him go and that I would never forgive him all my days. I turned to John Hickley and said, "I hope that's the last we ever see of that bastard." I can still see it all in my mind's eye, the combination driving off with Yosh on the back. I never saw him again, but I could never forget his gold teeth and evil slit eyes.

The accommodation down below in the hold was not too uncomfortable. A raised platform about knee high and six feet wide ran all the way round the hold. On it were several layers of rush matting, remarkably soft and quite comfortable to lie on. Everyone had about two feet of it in width as a berth, with all our bags and packs in a great heap in the centre. But there were no scuttles and we never saw the sun, and the only exercise we got was walking about in the gangways. Smoking was not allowed. The temperature was high and with so many human bodies in the enclosed space the atmosphere was not exactly exhilarating.

About noon the throb of the propellers indicated that we were on our way. After we got into the open water, secret compasses came out and we saw that we were going south-westerly. This meant Java or Singapore; Nippon would have required a course due north.

An excellent lunch by prison camp standards was produced. Though there was not very much of it, the rice was beautifully cooked and snow white and there was some succulent fish to go with it. After lunch we were allowed in groups to go up the ladder into a small saloon to smoke. The atmosphere became so full of smoke here that it was really not worth it. For supper they produced some rice and minced ham. That too tasted very good.

The men detailed to return the food tins and wash up the utensils after meals had to go on the upper deck to reach the galley. They reported that there was a small destroyer escorting us, but no land in sight. They also gave us the direction of the sun from which we could

Part of the docks at Tangjong Priok, the port of Batavia, before the war

determine the course to check the compass. This took a bit of working out as the sun in October was just south of the equator and we were about 5 degrees south in latitude. But we got a reasonable answer to show that the compasses were within a point or two despite the surrounding steel.

On the next two days we were allowed on deck for a quarter of an hour for fresh air. We were able to get a fair idea of the zigzag and mean course, which showed us to be going towards Batavia. The officer of the draft told us Java was our destination but just where in that island he did not know; but as he had often been wrong in the past we did not place much reliance on his word. I personally thought we would pick up more people at Batavia and then go north, though on the other hand, lack of tests for dysentery nullified the possibility of our going to Nippon.

We spent three days in that hold. It was not our idea of luxurious travel, herded down there like cattle, sweating continuously and with no room to move about. But this was "de luxe" compared with what other P.O.W.s were to experience.

We arrived in the afternoon of October 5th at Tangjok Priok (the port of Batavia), and about an hour after our arrival we were ordered to disembark. We were alongside one of the main jetties on which stood a group of very seedy looking Japanese Army officers with swords and no ties and their cricket shirt collars outside the lapels of their jackets; they were identifiable as army by the star on their caps and were quite a contrast from the Japanese naval officers who were always immaculately dressed. This boded no good for us as the Nip army had a pretty bad reputation.

So Java was our destination after all. Well, at least it was better than either Nippon or Singapore. The docks looked familiar yet somehow different. The pier opposite was the one we had left in *Exeter* to fight the battle of the Java Sea. The jetties looked deserted and unkempt with grass growing between the stones, which was strange.

What could be wrong with the place? Then suddenly I realised what it was. The harbour was empty, completely devoid of shipping except for our own transport and a salvaged wreck rotting with rust, and I was absolutely delighted. It was one of the most satisfying things I ever saw during the war, and I remember turning to my neighbour and saying, "Look, there's not a ship in the harbour. They've lost the war. The end is only a matter of time."

Batavia in peace time had been one of the major ports of the world. I think it was in the first twelve, and an average of sixteen ships a day used it. Out of it should have been flowing the wealth of that rich island to aid Nippon's war effort - nickel, tin, scrap, loot, quinine, besides rice, sugar and other foodstuffs. But the port was dead. Java was still producing. Vital raw materials were there for the taking, but there were no ships to collect them. From that moment onwards I had no doubt in my mind about the ultimate result of the war.

After landing, we embarked on lorries and were driven towards the town of Batavia. We knew the road well from the 1942 days before capture, and it was good to see familiar sights. It was just getting dark and the evening light made it all very colourful. After passing through part of the town we drove into a barracks which the Dutch told us was called the Cycle Camp. We could see British people at barrack windows and on office duties.

Outside the guardhouse we had to fall in to have our gear searched and be checked against certain particulars on the list. The senior Dutch colonel was arguing with the Nip officer at the table in Malay through an interpreter. The Nip was asking the colonel to sign, and to tell the rest of us to sign too, a statement that we would obey all Japanese orders and would on no account attempt to escape. The colonel was saying that he could not possibly sign such a statement.

The Nip officer was the adjutant of the camp. He was a tiny little man whose named proved to be Watanabe. He was young with a smooth, rather pleasant face which rather belied his nature, for he got very angry and eventually cracked the colonel hard over the head with a wooden baton he had in his hand.

The colonel was no young man - he was nearly sixty, and had been the senior officer in the Celebes. He was a quiet, retiring type, but did not lack courage when it was necessary. He said in Malay to the interpreter, "Ask this officer why he strikes another officer old enough to be his father? If he was not a coward he would strike me again." Watanabe was nonplussed. After much parleying, the colonel said that he would sign but reserved the right to state that it was done under pressure. All the Dutch followed suit.

This was a poser for me. Officers came to me and said, "What about it?" A few, whose voices had been heard on occasions but had never been noticed as coming forward to act, put on an air of great indignation, making out it was an inexcusable thing to sign.

I just said, "I don't trust the Nips to keep their word with us, so I don't consider my signature as binding if I put it on any bit of paper of theirs. They have just clouted the colonel on the head, and that's good enough for me. I think that can be construed as 'under duress'. I take full responsibility for your signing it and assure you that you are not bound by it. And don't sign in your normal signature."

That satisfied them and we all signed. It meant absolutely nothing. I signed in block letters. Few of the Nips understood English writing and I doubt if any understood the significance of it. One of our chaps put "U.D." for "under duress," after his signature, and it was never queried.

Later we found that others in the camp had refused to sign, so the Nips simply took the first working party of men returning from work and isolated them without water. They would get water when the signatures were completed. There was no further delay. In another camp, the officers refused and told the men to refuse. So Nips said, "All right, no food". Then after a few hours, the Nips went to the men and said, "The officers have now signed in order to allow you food. So you had better sign too". This was an utter fabrication, but when they had got the men's signatures they showed them to the officers and said, "All your men have signed, so if you don't you will be to blame if they starve to death". The officers signed.

About 8 p.m. we were marched through the camp and put into a barrack at the far end. We were told it was absolutely forbidden to contact or talk to anyone else in the camp, but as soon as the guards had left, numbers of British officers came in to welcome us. They said it was contrary to orders but as long as they stood near the door they would make a get-away if any guards came. They asked who we were and where we came from, and in a short while a general exchange of "dope" took place.

Cans of hot coffee arrived with all sorts of food from their canteen. We had never had such things for months, and this camp seemed a heaven compared with Macassar. Then the "pipe down" bugle went, and our friends departed back to their own quarters.

To crown it all, I went out of the door to wash, failed to see a monsoon drain and fell straight into it. I landed on the point of my left shoulder and jarred it badly. I climbed out feeling very sick.

9

The Cycle Camp

The first few weeks in this camp were pleasant and a great change from Macassar. We were not made to do any work and everything seemed peaceful. Food and drink seemed to dominate our lives. There was a canteen in the camp. It provided a variety of foodstuffs eggs, fruit, sugar supplied by a Javanese who no doubt had to pay the Nips a fee for the honour. The whole day would be given up to placing orders for food, collecting issues or buying coffee from a supply service which brought a kerosene tin of it round the camp every hour. We had been used to three meals a day and nothing extra, so at first our stomachs objected to the change of routine. We had very little money and spent it sparingly. Even so, an egg at five cents was a delicacy not to be missed.

The camp was about 1,500 strong - of mixed nationalities, both officers and men. There were about 200 British and Australian officers, Army and Air Force, and it was a great change for us to meet them after two and a half years of our own company. The senior officers were billeted in small rooms, the juniors in long barracks, and conditions were good though sometimes we were over-crowded - this was a transit camp and over 60,000 prisoners passed through it in three years.

About Christmas time, the big camp at Bandoeng, a hill station 120 miles south-east of Batavia, moved down to our camp, causing a great influx of officers, mostly R.A.F., with a few naval officers. Among them was Lieutenant Commander N.V. Thew, the C.O. of H.M.S. *Jupiter*, who, after his ship had been sunk, was fifty-two hours in the water. Six bad weeks had followed in Soerabaya from which his health had never really recovered. He had had his appendix out and was a chronic dysentery case. The R.A.F. called him "The Skipper" and believed he could "fix" anything, as apparently there was no source of supply that he did not know, be it pepper or tobacco, wireless news or money. He was magnificent in the way he helped his sailors and unstinting in his generosity.

He and some R.A.F. officers, including Wing Commander O.G. Gregson, were billeted in our room. "Greg" too was a great man. He had started his career by running away from home at the age of fifteen, when he joined the North Irish Horse as a trooper before the Kaiser War. He was a sergeant-major at twenty-one and had actually been in a cavalry charge, one of the last in history. In 1916 he transferred to the R.F.C., had flown a fighter aircraft on the Western Front and gained a commission. He had retired in 1927, emigrated to Western Australia and settled in Perth. Recalled in 1939, he had gone to Singapore and was in charge of the depot there when the Japanese attacked Malaya. He had lost his eldest son in H.M.A.S. *Sydney* in December 1941. After being transferred from Singapore to Java, Greg had been taken prisoner in March 1942.

Greg combined the strict discipline of the old-time cavalry officer with the high sense of duty and responsibility which were the characteristics of first line military units of the old days. He was very fond of the Navy and we all liked him. Our strict discipline and innate service loyalty appealed to him. A theosophist, deep thinker and sincere Christian, he was a great character and to me as fine a type of man as one could hope to meet.

Always sprucely turned out with R.F.C. buttons brightly polished and his cavalry moustache carefully clipped, he had a sergeant-major's voice and his words of command on parade were given in a magnificently stentorian manner. At the same time he was offensively cheerful, and his daily call of "It's a glorious morning" was famous.

The Bandoeng crowd, who had come from a well-organised camp with little discomfort and plenty of food, were rather shaken by the Cycle Camp where the canteen service had disappeared after our first three weeks. Those of us from Macassar took this in our stride, but the Java P.O.W.s, who were used to a canteen to supplement the rations, felt it badly.

We learned that food supplies for prisoners were greatly reduced throughout the Far East once Italy had abandoned the war. It was an order from Tokyo, presumably because the surrender of Italy was the first sure sign to the Nips that their own defeat was now a certainty. Garrisons throughout the Southern Regions were ordered to support themselves and send Japan everything that could be spared - provided there was shipping available. Though this naturally meant that we had to tighten our belts, it was reassuring to us to know that the tide had turned in the world outside.

Our rations were reduced to 4oz. of rice per day, with far less fish and meat and little or no canteen extras. And with this deprivation came an edict that as many P.O.W.s as possible were to be sent to work on railways, roads and airstrips in Singapore, in Thailand, in Sumatra, even in the great Nippon.

All the camp vegetable plots were dug up, our tomato and spinach crops destroyed, so that castor oil plants could be sowed instead; Nippon was very short of lubricating oil and there was a great castor oil drive going on throughout South-east Asia. We sowed three thousand plants in our camp. The Nips gave us minute instructions that the sprouting end of the seed must be placed uppermost and pointing towards Tokyo to ensure good growth! In fact most of them went in upside down, pointing towards Hell. But neither direction appeared to make any difference to the plants which grew very thickly and in nine months were about ten feet high and bearing their prickly nuts. They darkened the camp, encouraged mosquitoes and flies and were a bane to our existence.

The senior officers from Bandoeng, an R.A.F. wing commander named Nichol and a British Army colonel named Van der Post, soon took over command of all prisoners in the Cycle Camp; the Dutch colonel was worn out and wanted a rest and no one else was particularly keen to take on the job as it was a thankless one and pretty wearing. Besides, everyone else seemed scared stiff of the Camp Commandant, an army captain called Soni. The two from Bandoeng were afraid of no one. They took over, as they had done in their previous camp, and made a good job of it although they were not very popular at times with those who did not take easily to strong discipline.

Soni had been Camp Commandant from very early on. He was in the early thirties, usually very smartly dressed, with an imposing appearance and, when he chose, a cheerful disposition. But under it he was nothing but a swine. He spoke English quite well and understood it better, which made him quite dangerous as he could follow any conversation he overheard. There was no doubt about it that he hated the white man, the Dutch especially, as he considered them gutless, selfish and dishonest. The English he did not particularly admire, owing to our defeat in the Far East, and for our business acumen in Eastern commerce which he used to say was not entirely as honest as it might have been. And he hated women and for the obvious reasons we suspected.

He was of the bashing type. He used to get into frantic rages and cast loose with his fists, and was particularly bad at the full moon, though compared with Yoshida he was quite a gentleman. Which was perhaps why those of us from Macassar were not as afraid of him as most of the others in the camp, including his own guards. Whenever he came round to the camp the place resounded with shouts of "*kirei*" (Japanese for salutation) which was required by custom and order.

Usually most prisoners in his line of advance disappeared, and this I think tended to aggravate him. For one reason it showed fear, which the Japanese despised; for another it suggested that the people trying to avoid him were up to mischief; for a third that they could not bear the sight of him and were trying to insult him in their own quiet way.

In fact it was all three. We in the Navy from Maccasar were not particularly brave, but just thought this sort of thing stupid. So when Soni turned up we merely went on with whatever we were doing and saluted him as he passed. And everything was peaceful.

Soni was as brutal to his own men as he was to his captives. Once one of the guards stole a prisoner's watch during a search. A complaint was made to Soni, who fell in all the guards and asked for the culprit to step forward. Getting no reaction he went through their barracks and threw most of their kit out of the window without finding the watch. Again he paraded and harangued his men with no result. Then, prowling up and down in front of them, he suddenly picked on one of them and accused him of being the thief. He had guessed right because the man immediately confessed.

Dragging him out of the ranks, Soni began punching the man who took the battering on his face like a punch-ball, keeping his balance and coming back for more. By the end of the beat-up his face was an awful mess with both his eyes closed and several teeth out. He had to be taken to hospital, but was not there long. He was back on guard in three days still terribly damaged. Soni returned the watch to the owner with the assurance that none of his guards would ever steal again.

Soni left us in 1944 and went in charge of the women's camp at Tjideng, where he treated those prisoners shamefully. He did not hesitate to hit women in the face, and children went in terror of him. One day he kept everyone between the ages of two and seventy on parade from 9 a.m. to 4 a.m. the following day - nineteen hours. On another occasion he buried forty-eight hours' bread ration in a big hole in front of the entire camp. He used to give chocolate to his Alsatian dog in front of hungry children. As late as June 1945 he punished the administrative leaders, all women of high social standing, by clipping off their hair and shaving their heads in public. A little Korean guard called Noda, with great courage and taking his life in his hands, reported the case to Headquarters. Soni was relieved but, to our intense disgust, came as adjutant to the Japanese colonel of the Bandoeng camps where we then lived.

However, Soni was caught after the war. Before trying him, the military administrators sent him and his immediate subordinates up to Tjideng every day for several months to clean the sewers out of the camp in which he had behaved so badly. It must have been some consolation to hundreds of the women who were still there to see that overweening monster thus humiliated. Final retribution came at a war crimes trial at which he was condemned to death.

Once the tightening up orders came, Soni started the same blackmail tricks with the sick that we had experienced with Yoshida. Eventually he sent so many men out to work that there were insufficient left to do the camp work, and officers had to take over all these duties. Soon we completely ran the galleys, canteen, bakery, library, an outside garden, the woodchopping fatigues, the sanitation which included drainage and lavatories, and many other jobs. Actually, it was quite a good thing as it gave us all something to do. I was a woodchopper and as a manual worker got an extra 3/4oz. of rice. As a result, I put on several pounds in weight in four months, which brought me up to 11 stone 12 lb. Up to that time I had had no sickness at all and was reasonably fit.

Wood-chopping could of course be energetic - you poured with sweat, wielding an axe in the tropical heat - but we never allowed it to get out of hand. We did an hour's chopping after breakfast, then had a cup of tea and followed that with a little more chopping (if one was keen) and that completed the morning's work. On alternate days we did a further three quarters of an hour in the afternoon - if there was enough wood. The Nips were stingy with wood for fires.

A great thing about this camp was the supply of news. A number of secret wireless sets had been made and were being regularly worked. Some of these were most ingeniously designed and masterpieces of construction. One British set, made by two Royal Corps of Signals officers, could be transported from camp to camp in a space carved out of a wooden clog. The ear piece went in the wooden heel. It was normally kept in the false bottom of a stool which was casually left about. Practically every draft went out of camp with a set. One was built into three water bottles which could still contain water to conceal what was inside.

To work these sets the camp lighting circuits were tapped for power and the aerial - a fine wire round a mosquito net - was plugged in. The operator worked the set from inside the net which was easy to see out of but opaque to those looking in from the outside. A set in one camp was hidden in the rafters above the Japanese Commandant's office and remotely controlled. Another was stored in a man's wooden leg.

The officers who worked these sets, and transported them when camps moved, were very brave men. It was death to be caught with

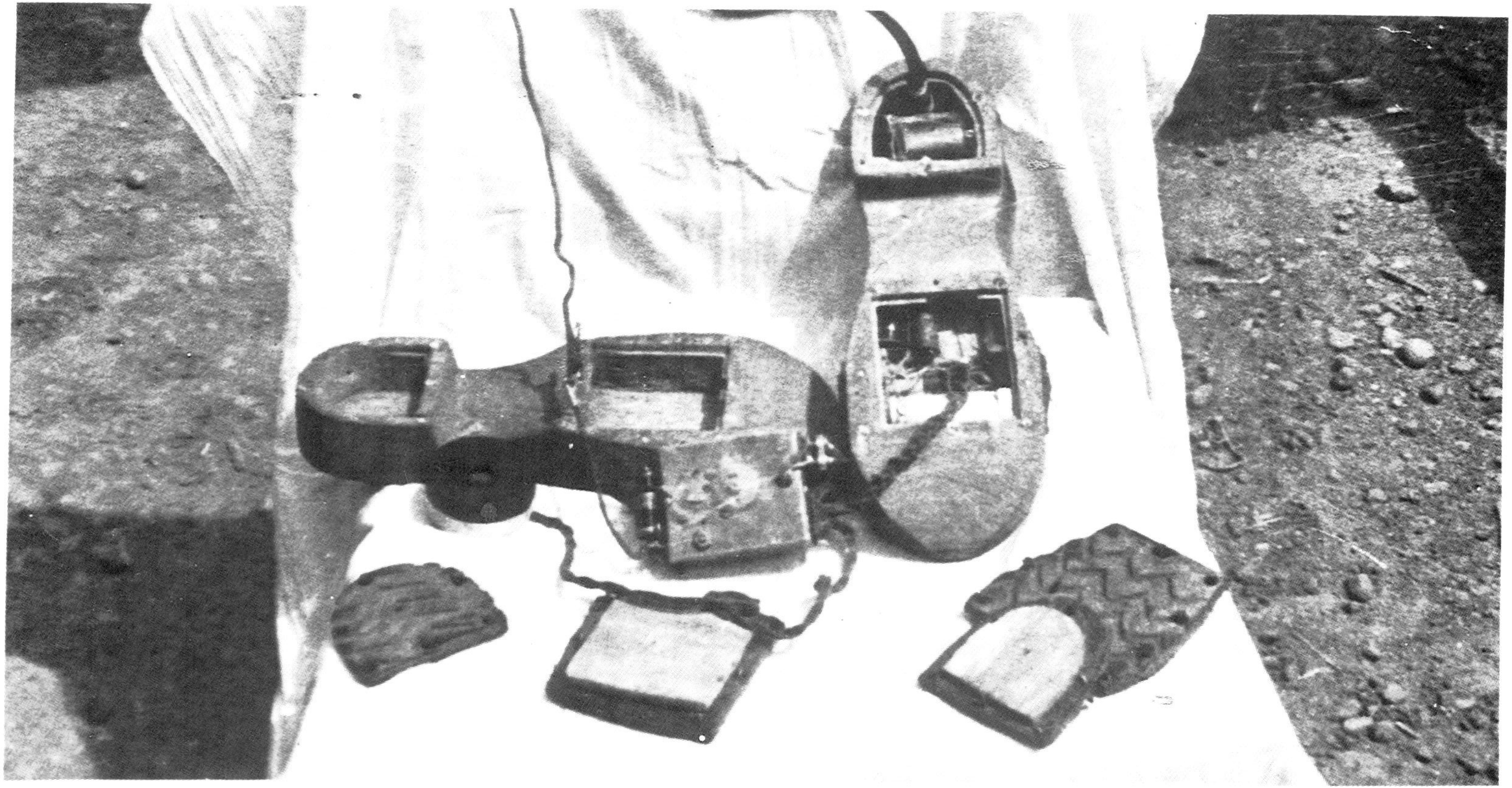

The "ice box", designed to fit into a pair of wooden clogs and used in Java to receive wireless news

one, and they all had many close shaves during searches. Their contribution to morale in providing news was incalculable and their audacity increased the thrill of receiving it. On one occasion during a prolonged parade, an officer went into barracks unobserved, got under his net and listened to a news broadcast with the Nips still outside.

As words like "radio", "wireless", "B.B.C." were known to the Nips and their informers in the camp, of which there were several, we used a code in which the set was referred to as the ice-box and news as ice-cream. The Nips knew we got news and suspected we had wireless sets, but fortunately never found one. The ice cream was disseminated through selected links, who only passed it on to other reliable links. Supply ceased to the link if any breach of security was suspected. This could be checked by putting out false news and seeing if it spread. I got my ice cream from an army colonel and was the link for the Naval officers from Macassar. I eventually got all of them into the circuit.

Another source of news was Japanese papers. These were stolen from the guards and once even from Soni's office; there was always someone in the camp who could read Japanese characters. One of these interpreters was hidden for years in the T.B. ward which was one of the places where the Nips never entered. I believe the Dutch had an ice-box there.

The Cycle Camp was wonderfully productive, almost self-sufficient. We ran a book-repairing shop, a tobacco factory in which cigars, cigarettes and pipe tobacco were made from the leaf, a soap factory, a paper factory, a workshop for making anything from a cooking ladle to a front axle, a carpentry shop, a tailor's shop for making and repairing clothes and uniforms both for P.O.W.s and guards, a clogmaking shop, a cobbler's shop, a pencil making factory, a nail factory, an artificial limb shop, a denture-making shop, a peanut butter factory, a jam factory, a basket and whisk shop, and there were others. There was practically nothing that could not be turned out in that camp by ordinary soldiers, sailors, airmen and civilians. Needless to say a lot of things were made clandestinely - components for ice-boxes, burglars' tools, knives and razors to name a few. The Nips provided some raw materials but most things were made out of old junk.

We made sufficient soap and cigarettes for all the camps, P.O.W. and civil, in the Batavia area - they accommodated about 90,000 prisoners. The Nips provided coconut oil and Dutch chemists and science professors made it into soap by obtaining the other basic ingredients from woodash and sea water. The soap was poor stuff - it burnt the skin if left on too long, but it was better than nothing. Lack of soap was one of the greatest hardships of prison life.

The tobacco was similar to the leaf we got in Macassar - low grade and very strong. Blind and disabled men worked in the cigarette factory. They used canvas rolling machines and were paid the same as those who went out on working parties - 10 cents a day. The Nips took their entire output, as they did that of the soap factory, and sold it to the prisoners and internees at an excessive profit. This we suspected was taken by those in command of the prison camps, and they must have made a fortune.

A fear that always hung over our heads was that of being sent away on a draft. This was almost tantamount to a death sentence for, apart from the danger of being torpedoed and sunk by our own submarines, the travel conditions, which got worse as the shipping shortage increased, were known to take a heavy toll of life. Then on arrival, the survivors had to face appalling conditions, often worse than Pomalaa, in the jungle camps to which they were finally sent.

One of the worst drafts that I know of arrived at the Cycle Camp in the autumn of 1944. They were mostly R.A.F. and Dutch and came from Haruku, one of the islands in the Ambon area east of Celebes. They started six hundred, crammed into the two holds of a small coaster which broke down on passage and eventually put into Macassar, where she remained anchored in the bay for forty days. Though the prisoners were dying in numbers every day, no effort was made to land them even temporarily at Macassar where accommodation and medical facilities were available. When repairs were complete they went on to Soerabaya, where they arrived sixty-eight days after leaving their original port of departure. They were then sent by train across Java to Batavia, a journey of some five hundred miles, which took another two days. Men were still dying in the train, their bodies being removed when they stopped at stations. Of the six hundred who started out, 327 died on that terrible journey, many of them through nothing more than lack of water.

Before that train arrived in Batavia, the Nips cleared the whole area within half a mile of the station and along the route to our camp; they were too ashamed to let the Javanese see how they cared for their prisoners. We were all confined to our barracks, but this did not prevent us seeing the draft march in. All were living skeletons, their skins a greyish colour, and though their heads were high they were just able to drag one leg after another; and these were the best of them, for 120 had gone straight to hospital. Only about 150 or 25 per cent had reached their actual destination - a pitiful sight and one I shall never forget.

I shall never forget too that such suffering could be inflicted by a people who regarded themselves a civilised nation and a major power. The Black Hole of Calcutta has a notorious place in history. The dark holds of that nameless Japanese coaster were no less ignominious.

Outgoing drafts from the Cycle Camp were usually between 1,000 and 2,000 strong. Before selection of a draft a parade of the whole camp would take place. This was always a very disturbing affair. We usually got wind of a draft several days ahead from those who worked in the Honshu or P.O.W. bureau, and it was always interesting to see how the dysentery rate suddenly rose in the camp; and some of these "cases" actually had all the dysentery symptoms.

Every prisoner had to be in one of four categories: A or fit; B, unfit but not a cot case; C, unfit; and D, disabled. I always said A as it was safest to be truthful. You never knew who was going on the draft - the fit or unfit. On one occasion they took all the "B" category men and sent them to another camp where they had to do everything themselves. This was a terrible camp as a result, as there were insufficient fit men to do even the cooking and hygiene duties.

When the camp paraded for the selection, the officers would be separated from the men; all being grouped by nationalities and again by categories. Soni would be very much in evidence, the performance taking anything up to six hours in the hot sun. He would do most of the selection himself, forming those selected into platoons of fifty, each under one junior officer. The total number of additional officers required for a draft would be about the same as the number required for an infantry battalion, so that for 1,000 they would probably pick another four captains, two majors, and one lieutenant-colonel, or equivalent ranks, with two or three doctors, a padre and perhaps a dentist.

Soni would not draft men who were vital to the running of his workshops and factory production lines, nor would he send men he liked. Anyone he disliked was soon picked, whether fit or unfit. The selection was very similar to that in the witch dance of Zaghool in *King Solomon's Mines*. Soni, like Zaghool, would arrive opposite a group, and look at them through his piercing slits. Then suddenly he would point at one and beckon him out, and the man fell in clear. To anyone he definitely did not wish to select he would say "Hoosh," and that fortunate one was moved to one side. Soni would also pick a number of reserves and weed them out later. It was always a terrible strain. Like most of the others who were tall and thin, I escaped being picked; the Nips, I believe, thought we were not very strong. The stocky, smallish types always caught the evil eye.

Once the draft was formed, they would be separated and kept in uncertainty for weeks and often months before departure. They would be paraded numerous times, checked and re-checked, changes made here and there, sick men replaced and others tested for dysentery and otherwise medically examined. These medical examinations were of course no more than being looked up and down by a passing Nip doctor while the prisoner stood with his shirt off and arms over his head. A few would be turned down to show that the doctor knew his job. The whole draft would then be supplied with boots, packs, blankets and other items of kit, but as the Nips never had enough of these the deficiencies would be made up from those in the possession of others in the camp - a real dirty trick and one which infuriated P.O.W.s who might have saved their money and stinted themselves of food in order to provide themselves with some particular item. Finally, there would be a dress rehearsal and at last we said good-bye.

Those leaving on a draft had to carry everything themselves, and it took a lot of ingenuity and planning to pack a lifesaving mosquito net, a change of clothes, a spare pair of clogs to save the boots, or even a mattress, besides treasured possessions. It was surprising how much one could accumulate over the years; prisoners are hoarders and cannot bear parting with anything. In the farewell parade the draft had to lay out on the road all the gear they had so carefully packed so that guards could search it.

When Soni was present there was always trouble. He would search some himself and he invariably scattered it in all directions or confiscated some vital article. It was sheer mental sadism. Directly the search was finished, men had to pack up all their gear, put it on their backs and be ready in about five minutes, while the guards who were always in a hurry charged round with their rifles shouting "Lekas, lekas" (quick, quick). As a result many oddments were left on the road, and after the draft had left the Nips would collect them up and put them in the store for the next issue. It was a mean trick and quite typical of the things they did.

Throughout 1943 and 1944 drafts went out. There was one to Malaya in 1943, one to Sumatra in the spring of 1944, one to Nippon in May 1944, another to Sumatra in August 1944, one to Flores with Indians some time later.

One morning at the dawn muster a Nip who worked in the camp office came to the British officers' platoon and said he wanted to see those of the rank of lieutenant. He selected two, John Hickley and Philip Cranefield, and told them they would be going on draft at eleven o'clock. They had suddenly been condemned to leave their friends and go to an unknown destination; no one knew at the time where the drafts were bound.

Their ship was later sunk thirty miles south of Nagasaki by an American submarine. Out of 1,000 in the draft only about 300 were saved, fortunately these two among them, after fourteen hours in the water. A number of Australians were lost in that draft as well as one of our naval doctors. The news always came back to us through the P.O.W. bureau.

By July 1944 the number of P.O.W.s in Java had dropped to about 8,000. Of these 1,500 were officers, mostly Dutch. At least 4,000 of the total were in very poor health, so obviously it would not be long before the officers went in the body of the draft. The Japanese policy was to draft men according to their skills and ability to be productive. The first to go had been those with technical qualifications - fitters, mechanics, electricians and the like. Unskilled but fit men had then followed, and by now all they had left were the unskilled crocks, plus those who had been permanently in camp administrative jobs, the key men in Soni's workshops and factories, and the officers.

The officers had not been made to work quite like the men. Though they had forced us into doing the camp chores, they regarded this as voluntary work; it was never official Japanese policy to treat officers like coolies as to have done so might have undermined the position and prestige of their own officers. We were therefore considered unproductive and left to near the end - just one category above the sick and dying. But with thousands already gone it seemed that our own turn was not far off.

In August a draft of 2,200, of which all were Dutch except for 120, left for Sumatra. This was a terrible draft as 75 per cent were unfit, some barely able to walk with their gear. A large number were Dutch Home Guard from Batavia, most of them civilians of high social status - managers, university professors and the like. They had been treated as ordinary soldiers and not as officers, and had had a bad time really as they were oldish men. One of these was the senior French professor at Batavia university, who had taught me French twice a week. He was about 6 ft. 7 in., near sixty, about four stone under-

-weight and reminded me curiously of a poplar tree. I used solemnly to give him a guilder a month for his lessons, and with this he could buy some cigarettes. There was I paying him 8d. per week for French conversation. It was rather pathetic.

The ship carrying this draft was sunk on its way to Sumatra. Out of 2,200, some 1,500 were lost, including my French master. It was all very sad, yet the sinking of this ship saved the lives of the rest of the officers. Later in September, she was due to return to Java to pick us up and take us north to Japan. If Java was overrun, the Japanese were making quite certain that no prisoners would be recaptured. The ship did not return so we could not leave until another one arrived. In the interval of waiting the Americans recaptured the Philippines and cut the last line to Nippon, and we had to stay in the Southern regions.

The Nips, seeing that an invasion might well take place to clear the way for the assault on Singapore, decided to remove all P.O.W.s from coastal towns to more secure places inland; but in the hope of saving the coastal towns from bombardment, they put the civil internees there.

At the end of October 1944, when their navy had been finally crushed off Leyte, a great general-post of P.O.W.s and internees commenced. The P.O.W.s now concentrated in Batavia started to move up to Bandoeng, while the civilians in East Java were brought west, and most of those in the Bandoeng civilian camps were sent to Batavia.

10

The Car Episode

I left Batavia on October 27th, 1944 in a party of 800 officers and travelled by train up to Bandoeng. Before we left, our gear was searched as usual, but fortunately this was only cursory as quite a few people had ice-boxes. Like those on overseas drafts we had to carry everything we possessed, and as we marched the mile to the station I balanced my roll-up mattress, sleeping mat and blanket on my chest and my stuffed haversack on my back.

A Nip colonel named Kawabe was on the station to see us off. He was the officer in charge of camps in Batavia, a nasty little wretch with an unsavoury reputation. The train was composed of coolie carriages and we were pretty crushed.

The Dutch were all apprehensive about leaving Java. The island was "home" to them. Their families were here and they naturally wished to remain. So there was a definite sigh of relief when the train started and we went inland instead of to Tangjong Priok.

I enjoyed this trip more than anything else in Java. In two and a half years I had barely been outside the prison camps and then only while on transit. This was a whole day out travelling through a most attractive countryside, through paddy fields and wooded valleys and gorges, then climbing up and up and round and round mountain slopes covered with terraced cultivation. The rice was a brilliant green and most beautiful to view. When the train stopped at stations the guards insisted on having the shutters closed so that we could not see the names of the towns through which we were passing. They were quite unsuccessful in this respect and we managed to note all the places. In any case the Dutch knew their own country backwards.

It took all day to cover the 120 miles from Batavia to Bandoeng. At intervals the engine would have to re-fuel with wood and take in water; there was no coal in Java and the Japanese were running the railways on Java teak much to the disgust of the Dutch. It would take decades for the plantations to recover.

We arrived at Bandoeng at 5 p.m. and had a march of about three miles to our new camp. When we arrived, we found about 700 Dutch from other camps already in occupation, having arrived about two hours before. We were racked with thirst by this time, having had nothing to drink for nearly eleven hours. Lack of water in the tropics is debilitating and we were somewhat exhausted. The Dutch in the camp produced some buckets of water and we drank heavily. They had had the same experience and were able to appreciate our needs.

It was nearly dark by the time we had sorted out the accommodation available. The camp was about three hundred yards long by one hundred and fifty yards wide, full of barracks and odd buildings. It had been a P.O.W. camp in 1942 and before that a cavalry barracks, but it had been stripped by P.O.W.s on the orders of the Nips. The job had been so well done that absolutely nothing remained in any room or barrack - not an article of furniture of any sort, not a single electric light, not a door or window fitting. Just walls, floors and roofs and nothing else. There were five small taps as washing facilities for all 1,500 of us. In the galley, there were two large rice steamers and a few odds and ends.

We lived on the floor in that camp for six months. Various additions were made to the galley and wells were dug to provide water for washing. Everyone was very crowded. Five other officers and I shared a room twelve feet square and that was comfortable compared with the way people lived in some of the big barracks. In time we got some electric bulbs so that we had one light in each room and about four per barrack.

We were pretty tired that first night when we turned in about ten o'clock, but no one slept for hours. The bugs came out of the walls in their battalions to feast on us; they had had nothing to live on for two years so were pretty hungry. By midnight I was driven to distraction, and went to a concrete path outside where I took over eighty bugs off my mosquito net in the moonlight before settling down again.

This was a bad camp. We never got outside and being crowded with so many others in such a confined space made life almost intolerable. The climate, at 2,200 ft., was delightful - warm and sunny all day and cool at night. But the cooler conditions and rarefied air made us even more hungry than we were. We did get a little extra rice but it was far from being enough, and the general health of the camp went steadily down as we lost weight at an average rate of two or three pounds per month. By April I was down to 10 stone 12 lb. There was nothing to do all day for the majority of us as only a limited number worked in camp services. To occupy ourselves we studied languages and other subjects. I learnt Dutch in this period using several teachers. I did a lot of French too, mostly with a young Dutch Army lieutenant whom I taught English in return.

At night we either gave lectures or listened to them; we in the Navy were much in demand especially by Dutch and Australians who were keen to learn about war at sea. I sometimes used to lecture twice or three times a week. We had no books of reference, so had to prepare a lecture pretty thoroughly beforehand by checking on points of detail with others, and as some of the audience were foreigners, we had to speak slow, distinct and grammatical English without using slang. This in fact gave us good experience, and the improvement of our lecturing abilities was one of the good things that came out of being in the "bag". The principal subjects I spoke on were "The Functions of the Royal Navy in War", "A review of Naval Operations in the Present War", "Contraband Control", "Torpedo Bomber v. Battleship", and "Training of Naval Officers".

In December 1944 I commenced a series of instructional lectures - compulsory instruction for the sub-lieutenants. I remember telling the subs - they had been the midshipmen when I was "snottie's nurse" in the ship - that it appeared highly probable or at least likely that we might be free within six months and that this interval should be spent in preparing for our return to the service. Morale and optimism were very high among the British officers at this time, and the subs were keen students. Everyone did about two hours a week on navigation with an instructor officer, and two hours general seamanship as arranged by me. Special lectures were also given on shiphandling and victualling and other subjects. Everyone benefited by the mental effort required and it employed time. Every Thursday evening I had a personal *téte-à-téte* with Ian Forbes on how to run a destroyer, down to the most minute detail. We would intersperse this with things on life in general. They were great evenings.

Ian Forbes, a young lieutenant of twenty-five, had on his own initiative taken over the duties of senior officer of the junior officers' barracks. There were about 160 people involved, from all three services, and composed of British, Canadians, New Zealanders, and a few Americans, of all ages up to sixty. Many were civilians from Malaya, who had volunteered after the invasion and had only been in uniform a few weeks before being captured. They had not got the service background, and to command this medley lot, to deal with all their troubles and moans, and to organise their billets, food, duties and so on, required personality and leadership of a very high order. Ian was a very fine officer and he stood no nonsense. He was not very popular in the first month or two, but he knew what he wanted and he was going to get it. After two months, he had them all right under his thumb, and the majority admired, respected and appreciated him.

The period in this uncomfortable camp was made more endurable by the excellent news of the war in Europe and in the Pacific; the supply of news was excellent, several wireless sets operating. But the setback during the Ardennes offensive at Christmas 1944 was withheld from general distribution in order to maintain morale. The death of President Roosevelt too was depressing at a time when victory in Europe was imminent.

The Nips were on the whole quiet in this camp except on an occasion I shall call the car episode. Alongside our camp was a narrow no-man's-land which separated us from a civilian boys' camp. In this strip the Nip guards had hidden a car in a shed. They had even wiped out the tyre marks so that the Kempetai and Headquarters would not find out. I suppose the Camp Commandant wanted it for escape purposes when the time came. However, some Dutch fighter pilots discovered this car while out in a working party, and in the course of the next few weeks pretty well took it apart. Much of a car was useful, and by the time they had finished with it only the bare shell remained. But they did not hide their traces very well, and moreover they removed a revolver and ammunition which they found in the car. There was nothing tactical or patriotic about this looting; it was not just a sabotage attempt. The pilots' motives were venal for, it was said, they sold what they had stolen at exorbitant prices to their comrades. The tyres for instance made excellent rubber shoes. A pair of these fetched as much as eighty guilders (£10).

Eventually in March the guards in the boys' camp discovered the remains of the car and accused us. Our guards denied the charge and said that our camp was composed solely of officers who did not steal. The other guards did not accept this statement and suggested a combined search in the camp. We unfortunately got no wind of this at all, and at the morning muster one day we were retained on parade while the Nips went through our barracks. All they found were headlamp reflectors but that was sufficient. Four Dutchmen were incriminated and were removed forthwith to the cells. The Nips then demanded their four accomplices; they said there were eight in the gang, and they were right, which rather suggested the presence of informers even in an officers' camp.

Two more owned up but they still wanted another two. Then next day another, who was seriously implicated but too afraid to come forward, was forced to confess. The last one was quite yellow and refused, and eventually a companion only slightly implicated offered himself as a victim. It was a brave and unselfish act. The Nips were now reasonably satisfied.

They did not appear to mind so much about the car, but were very worried about the pistol, which they were determined to have back. Obviously they would get into serious trouble if they could not explain its loss as their regulations concerning firearms were every bit as tight as ours.

At first the eight denied all knowledge of the pistol, but on being promised no extra punishment they told the guards where they could find the bits of it. The gun had been dismantled, some of the parts being used for various purposes, and the remainder thrown down a sewer. These were recovered and the guards were satisfied that it was not being kept for use against them.

Meanwhile our canteen had been stopped; which meant no extras for any of us in the way of fruit, sugar and tobacco, and without which life was miserable. The victims were on low diet.

A few days later, when I was taking my afternoon walk, I saw the guards working on these wretched men. They had lined them up in front of the guardhouse, and six Nips with crow-bars and clubs were in front and behind them bashing them over the head, shoulders and legs. I turned away nauseated. I was quite white when I got back to my room and a Canadian pilot said, "What's wrong with you?"

"Kasiyama and his friends are beating up the car fellows," I said. "I think it's as nasty a scene as I have yet witnessed."

I believe they kept it going for about forty-five minutes, until all the accused were pretty well out on the road and covered in blood. They were then thrown back into the cells, from which they were released after about six weeks. All youngsters, they came out looking old and broken men.

Then came the punishment for the rest of us. We had already had no canteen for three weeks, by which time nearly everybody had exhausted his stocks kept for such emergencies. I was down to one cigarette per day. Worse, I had no sugar left and this was almost an essential addition to the bread which was made of tapioca flour. But now the Nips suddenly ordered all foodstuffs in the camp to be taken to the guardhouse, and it was then announced that there would be no food for forty-eight hours.

When we in the British contingent heard this we roared with laughter, but the faces of the Dutch were a sight for the gods - they could never bear missing their food. We then saw our rice dinner taken round to the boys' camp which pleased us as throwing it away would have been criminal.

But that was only part of it. At noon that day we were all ordered to sit on our bed spaces and meditate on the grossness of our crimes. We were not to talk, walk, lie down, sleep, smoke or read. We just had to sit in silence, and being in a room opening on to the road my room mates and I had to sit it out; we could not place lookouts as some of the others did.

Curiously enough the Nips left us alone, except for a few desultory patrols. It was of course their Asiatic dislike of being unpopular, and rather than see and feel our hate and disgust they kept away.

By nightfall we were all suffering from the effects of starvation. Although the temperature was about 75°F we were all very cold and shivering, and some people were vomiting. I put on all the clothes I had and still felt cold. Darkness was cover for movement, for talking and smoking - not that we had many cigarettes. I made up three out of the tobacco dust remaining in my stock, and they helped to ease the gnawing hunger pangs. It was difficult to sleep for long periods during the night.

At daybreak an evil little face appeared in our window. It was that of Kasiyama, the chief Korean guard, a nasty little man who spoke English well and was a very dangerous customer. He made a number of gloating remarks like "*Tidah makan*" (no food) which were received in icy silence. He then tried to be ingratiating, and we told him what we thought of the punishment and the Japanese.

"*Nippon tidah bagoos*" (Japanese no good), we repeated.

He took it in good humour and as he went off he said something to the effect that the Nips were not so bad as we thought, from which we were left with the impression that we would get our dinner that day.

The thought of another twenty-four hours without food was not exactly exhilarating, though by now I had become accustomed to the pangs and was confident of being able to stick it out. However, soon after that the cooks were sent to the galley to prepare the midday meal. The Nips had relented.

They said, "Punishment was for two days - yesterday and today. Two days now over. You will have dinner."

Actually I rather think we just wore them down with our silence; being hated so virulently got too much for them. The dinner at midday was magnificent. It needed to be.

We left this camp soon after this incident. Our captors considered it necessary to have us in a place even more secure than our present camp, since the Australians were working down through the islands - New Guinea, Morotai, Borneo, and an assault on Java did not seem unlikely, though I personally did not think this would take place. Rather, I expected an assault on Singapore, then a sweep north-east towards China in order to gain ports and air bases for the final assault on Japan.

Despite the great distances and effort involved in these strategic considerations, we had no doubt in our own mind that the war would finish that year. The lack of shipping and the severing of their sea communications had isolated Japan from most of her conquered territories, and there were strong signs too of defeatism and despondency among the Nips whose discipline had seriously deteriorated. They were drinking more and the Korean guards had started playing a double game. These guards no longer hesitated to keep us informed of the main news and even of Japanese policy.

Not that we admired the Koreans for it. They could be very pleasant and seemed of better breeding than their Japanese equivalents, but they had all the nasty habits of the Nips with very few of the good ones. Most were well educated men, who had been brought out to Java for administrative and economic posts in the newly occupied territory, but on arrival had been incorporated into the garrison troops much to their disgust. The majority, forming an organisation called Gunzuoko, had been posted as guards for the P.O.W. and internee camps.

They had been deceived by their masters, and now realised they would also have finally to fight for Japan in a hopeless cause in remote islands against overwhelming opposition. They were not permitted to hold any rank and a Japanese sergeant, usually of the basher type, was in charge of each set of guards in the camps. Their only time off was half a day a week. They lost all along the line, but that did not excuse them for the brutal way in which they treated us earlier on when it still looked as though Japan might survive. The man I have mentioned, Kasiyama, was as bad as any Nip.

At this time, April 1945, it looked to us that the Japanese policy in Java was to make Bandoeng a military stronghold, inside of which they would keep their main force and the P.O.W.s. If this was so it would be a pretty difficult job to take the town except by a massed parachute attack, as it lay in a hollow and could only be entered by a couple of roads running through easily defended passes. We estimated that the Japanese had about 20,000 troops in Java, most of which were in the Bandoeng area. We were hopelessly out in our estimate. At the capitulation it was a shock to find they had more like 70,000.

In April, the British camp leaders set up a highly secret organisation to take the initiative in the event of an Allied invasion. Nothing was committed to paper, and only six officers of which I was one, were in the secret. The scheme was designed to cope with any attempt by our captors to liquidate us when an Allied landing was made on Java. It would also support a mass breakout to join our friends.

Three platoon leaders were selected - two wing commanders and myself, all three of us as being physically fit and experienced in command. Each was to select his own platoon, and only fit young men were to be chosen. Three platoons were just about as much as we could form in the camp at the time; most of the others being considered too sick, old or unreliable. No. 1 Platoon composed mostly of strapping Australians with some R.A.F. wireless experts, was to make a forced march of fifteen miles, and capture the wireless station at Malabar, and thus get in contact with the Allied forces. No. 2 Platoon was to be responsible for getting hold of arms and food from local supplies. It was formed of R.A.F. pilots, all young men and full of dash. My platoon, drawn mainly from the Navy and made up to strength by senior officers who were reasonably fit, was to be responsible for the defence of the camp against any attempt, especially by the local natives to assault it. As there were several officers of the other services who were senior to me, it was agreed that questions of rank would be waived in the event of an emergency.

We found out and memorised the sleeping billets of all members of our respective platoons, so that we could rouse them quickly and easily at night. We formed them into sections in our own minds in order to avoid committing anything to paper. The Nips were terrified and suspicious of any form of conspiracy, and the sentence for anything of this sort was execution. None of the other officers concerned, even those selected for the platoons, knew of the scheme, and it remained secret to the end. It was never used but it was a wise precaution. The possibility of some incident occurring which might lead to mass liquidation was always present in 1945. This caused us the gravest concern.

Towards the end of April more P.O.W.s came up from Batavia. They told us it was common knowledge that all those who remained in the Cycle Camp would soon be coming up to Bandoeng, together with the sick from the hospitals. This was bad news as it meant that the overcrowding would be simply frightful. We also heard that the discipline of the Japanese in Batavia was going to pieces, and that the Korean guards in the camp were co-operating with the P.O.W.s in blatant black market transactions. The whole camp seemed to have turned into one big racket, and apparently a young R.A.S.C. lieutenant, a non-regular officer who was commanding the prisoners there, was having a very difficult time keeping the Nips quiet and the men in order.

All of which confirmed our belief that the war would end that year. Germany was at the end of her tether, and with her out of it the downfall of our captors could not be long delayed. But there were many signs of a forthcoming move for ourselves. It was to be a local move and on foot, but you could never be certain. Often the Nips put out false rumours for security reasons. However, this time it seemed a move was definitely on.

It came on April 27th and was a remarkable achievement of organisation, both by the Nips and the prisoners. We shifted everything out of the camp - galley gear complete, workshop equipment, furniture, rice stocks, sick, hospital gear (little though it was), and ourselves with our belongings in one day. We did not miss a meal either. We left in the late afternoon, and marched one and a half miles to our new abode, which was a bit further out of the town and away from any habitation. I remember thinking to myself that I had been nineteen months in Macassar, thirteen in the Cycle Camp and six months in cavalry barracks; each period getting less. It seemed that this mathematical retrogression was bringing me nearer and nearer the end, and curiously enough I stayed two and a half months in this camp, two in the next, a fortnight in the next, a week in the one after and just one day in the final one. It was not far wrong.

11

Bamboo

The new place was ghastly. It was a reformatory, a Borstal, built to house four hundred Javanese juvenile delinquents. It was two hundred yards square and completely surrounded by a 20-foot wall. In previous camps, the fences were of tinplate or atap (palm-thatch), but here we were literally inside the four walls of a pretty secure prison with barred windows in the rooms high up near the ceiling, and being in it was extremely depressing.

The sanitary arrangements were lamentable. There were twenty-two W.C.s of the squatting type open to the public, and that was all. All right perhaps for four hundred, but we were now over two thousand, and within a month another 1,800 came up from Batavia, officers and men of all categories. It meant that from the 3,800 people there was a continual queue for the W.C.s, and we had to detail officer pickets to control the traffic. Dysentery patients had a doctor's chit and could go to the top of the queue. After using a W.C. each person had to draw a bucket of water and use it to flush it manually. At night before lights out it was nothing to find 120 ahead of you in the queue for the urinals which we built.

I seldom took the trouble to join this but would wait till it had eased off at about 10.30 or later; I felt it did not matter whether you used the place before turning in or not as you always had to make a visit in the night. Excessive micturition was one of the effects of our low diet, and the quantity of rice we ate added to it. Pap-rice porridge would increase bladder activity even further, making it necessary to urinate every half-hour for about two hours after eating the stuff. We had it very badly in Macassar, where one night I took a census of the visits made by 500 men and found the number in excess of 1,200. There was an almost constant clip-clop of wooden clogs along the concrete covered walk. Throughout my captivity I went through only seven nights without turning out. If the temperature dropped at all visits increased, so that five times in the night was not abnormal. You got used to it but it was an awful curse, especially when we were billeted so close together that it meant crawling on all fours between mosquito nets and stepping over bodies. In Batavia I was near the door, and in Bandoeng by a ground floor window, but the latrines were always some way off and in the monsoon rains it was not easy to keep dry.

This camp was called the L.O.G. which stood for Land Opgerveld Gymnasial, or State Correction School. The barrack rooms were built into the walls, with one set of buildings in the middle. To increase the accommodation we had to build two tiers of wooden platforms in each barrack, and on these as well as the floor each person had a sleeping space of about two feet with three feet of head room. In this space you ate and slept and kept all your belongings. In my barrack, about the size of a tennis court, there were 280 British officers. Today if I offered guests the same accommodation I could put up about 200 in my home, which is a four bedroomed house.

Those who had the berths on the floor got all the dirt from the traffic up the centre gangway. In these it was just possible to sit up, but it was too dark to read even by day. They were known as the dog kennels. Those on the centre tiers - the chicken coops - were clear of dirt but got little light; and they were continually being disturbed by traffic to and from the tier above. The top row, or birds' nests, had light from the window, and even a view out over the wall, but to reach them one had to climb up a vertical support with notches on it. These birds' nests were the berths to have. Three vertical sets were allocated to our group of senior officers, nine in number, and we drew for choice. I drew first and got the five of clubs. I reckoned I was for a dog kennel, but strange to say seven people drew cards below mine. So I got a birds' nest, which was heaven compared with the lower tiers, particularly for me as I was too tall to sit upright on either of them. On top I could sit up and read and move about as I liked. Clambering up and down to make the nightly visits was a difficult operation though.

In Macassar I had never been sick, and in Batavia only one day with internal disturbances. At the previous camp I had had one bout of dengue when on the last day my temperature reached 105° before suddenly dropping to 97° as the attack passed. I had avoided malaria, dysentery, and serious beri-beri - we all had slight beri-beri. Why I was so fortunate I do not know, except that I took care of my health, used a mosquito net and took regular exercise. Also I can eat anything.

But now in May 1945, just after we arrived at this camp, I got an attack of bronchitis and was ill for nine days on the floor. The tiers had not then been built and I remember it was embarrassing at night when the drop in temperature made me cold and my violent panting woke everyone up. I could not lie down as this caused immediate loss of breath, so I had to sleep half sitting up. It was a depressing period.

With thousands of people plodding about in the camp the centre grass plots were ploughed up, and heavy rains turned them into a quagmire. The place was so bad that the Nips decided it should be paved with stones, and moreover that the officers should do the work. The camp had been built on a swamp and the surrounding land filled in with stones. We were to get stones from this reclaimed swamp, about eight hundred of us being put to this daily. There were strong "union" rules about this work. One trip per hour was considered the maximum that anyone should do. During that hour he should poke about in the ground, sit and talk or just wander round with the air of one working but actually enjoying the view. Between these activities he could pick up the odd stone and put it in the sack he helped to fill with three others. Then, when at last it contained about 50lb. of stone, he with the three, each holding one corner, would slowly bring it into the camp and dump the load. By keeping a constant relay of "fours" going in and out of the gate, the Nips thought we were working very hard, but in fact no single officer accounted for much more than about 50lb. in a five hour day. However, even at that rate, in forty days eight hundred officers moved over 700 tons of stone, which we pounded down in the mud to make two fine parade grounds.

The virtue of this job was that it got us out into the fresh air and sunshine, and the view which we found so distracting was in fact a grand sweep of jungle and cinchona clad mountains. It also cleared the camp for some hours every day which was healthy and gave the hygiene squads and those cleaning barracks a chance to keep the place sanitary. Still, none of us liked picking stones out of a swamp and carting them on to a parade ground. It was coolie work and the Nips had used great craft in getting us to do it.

The Nip sergeant-major of the Bandoeng camps at this time was a basher named Mori, but better known as Bamboo after the weapon he normally used. He was very big for a Japanese, with enormously broad shoulders, a beautifully built man and as fit as a horse. In one camp he had carried 440lb. of rice on his back uphill to demonstrate how men should work. At Haruku, a small island in the Ambon Group he had earned for himself an unsavoury reputation. In that camp 700 out of 2,000 had died, either there or on transit back. They had been sent to build an airstrip out of coral, but first had had to build their own camp. The bulldozers for the landing strip had broken down, so the P.O.W.s had to do all the work by hand. They took nine months to build a 1,500 yard runway, breaking down the coral with hammers and chisels and carting it as we had done stones. Most of this draft were R.A.F. and all had dysentery before starting. Over 300 died in the first few months.

Bamboo could be very pleasant and amusing, but once angry became very dangerous. One of his specialities was hitting prisoners in the face with the buckle of his Sam Brown, swung with all his strength. It could and did tear men's faces to pieces. With a club of any sort he was a positive menace. I lived with an officer from Haruku, and his stories of Bamboo were simply frightful. Now this inhuman brute was our chief executive boss. He was always spotlessly turned out and rode a motor cycle with great dash; it was a new toy for him and he was like a schoolboy with it.

We had no trouble with Bamboo for some time, the camp being run by the Korean, Kasiyama, who had been under him at Haruku. Kasiyama was terrified of Bamboo, who would beat him up too if anything went wrong. Bamboo hated and despised Kasiyama, and did not mind telling him. So Kasiyama took it out on the prisoners. Apart from venting his spleen, he felt that by keeping his P.O.W.s in submission he kept himself out of trouble with Bamboo.

Kasiyama was about the only guard I met who could count men and get the muster correct. But this was his only saving grace. His knowledge of English and Malay made him particularly dangerous as on dark nights he would disguise himself in the clothes and clogs of a prisoner and go snooping round the camp. He listened to conversations hoping for a lead to the various illicit activities that were going on, such as food smuggling, gambling (strictly forbidden) and the like. He used to say, "I know all that goes on in this camp. I see and hear everything." In addition he was a sadist and instigated some of the worst beat-ups in this camp. Everyone hated him.

We had one memorable scene in the L.O.G. One day - it was June 18th, 1945 - an order came that all P.O.W.s were to parade at 5 p.m. with all men acquainted with repairs to ships, machinery and aircraft in each unit fallen in ahead of them.

"To Hell with this," we said, but duly fell in, the Dutch with only a token number of technicians in position, but the British officers without a single one. Then Kasiyama came round looked at our group, and asked where our candidates were. We replied that we had none who qualified as such.

"Bloody crazy! Bloody, bloody crazy!" Kasiyama screamed. (He knew all the swear words).

He then directed that all the British would have to fall in outside the administration office in alphabetical order, while he checked each against his card to see whether or not he was lying. We did not like the sound of this as obviously such people as engineer officers in the Navy, and R.A.F. officers could be considered as knowing something about repairs to ships, machinery or aircraft. However, I primed all naval officers to say that we were seamen and that our repairs were done for us by dockyards, which was true. One engineer officer arranged to say that he was only an engine room watchkeeping officer and being ex-R.N.V.R. was not trained in repair work.

Kasiyama duly started. But he only got as far as the Bs when a great roar from the direction of the gate announced the arrival of Bamboo. He just stood there, clenching his fists and waving his arms. "Kas-ai-ma! Kas-ai-ma!" he yelled. It was the way he pronounced Kasiyama's name.

The Korean went over and got what appeared to be a terrific strip torn off him by Bamboo, who was obviously very displeased. This naturally delighted us - it was dog eat dog, and even better, for Bamboo then came forward a few steps and in broken English shouted at us, "Goh! Goh awaee! All men goh awaee!"

We went without further bidding, but unfortunately there was a bit of a rush into our compound with lots of laughter and noise. "Kasiyama's for it, good-o!" "Serve the little bastard right!" "What a party!" "Well, we've got away with that one!" and so on. Some people were quite hilarious.

Something told me this was a mistake, and I said as I walked back with some friends, "There's going to be a row about this. All that noise and laughter. Bamboo won't stand for it. They've both lost face and they'll have to regain it. Look out for some fireworks now." The pyrotechnics I prophesied came almost at once.

The whole camp was still fallen in, and we had barely regained our position, when a messenger came up to say that all the British senior officers, thirty-five of us, were required outside the guardhouse. As we arrived, we saw our Camp Commander, Wing Commander Alexander who had been ordered to stay behind, being set on by Bamboo. He was going for him with both fists, knocking him down, dragging him back to his feet and doing it again. He had obviously been thoroughly beaten up and was white as a sheet. Then, when he could barely stand and looked as if he was about to faint - he was being held up by his own adjutant - Bamboo temporarily suspended the assault. Actually he had broken Alexander's jaw.

Next we fell in in three ranks; I in the rear rank on the left. About six Korean guards were there, with Kasiyama fawning round Bamboo and the latter himself in a furious rage. Bamboo came and stood in front of us and jabbered away in Japanese, Kasiyama translating bits of it into English. The gist of it was that an order of the Japanese had been disobeyed and it was obvious that we, the senior officers, had instructed the others not to volunteer their names for the repair work. It was all our fault. Actually the decision was an unanimous one, and we had influenced no one.

Bamboo then took off his tunic and stood there, a massive gorilla of a fellow in a soft peaked cap, white singlet, loose breeches and jack boots. Then, pointing at the right hand man of the front rank, he said something that sounded like "*Hai*" and obviously meant "Come here".

The officer stepped forward to be met as he arrived within striking distance of Bamboo with a straight right in the face. He went down like a ninepin but got up again and regained his place. The next man was then called out and struck, then the next and so on along the front rank and back along the second rank. Some went down, some remained standing.

One of the older types who had been a boxer knew how to withdraw his head that little bit which takes the edge off a knock-out blow, and he stood it all right. At one time I saw five officers of the rank of commander or lieutenant-colonel on the ground.

Then half-way through the act Greg stepped out in front and very courageously shouted out, "Hi! Stop this. What's all the trouble? What order have we disobeyed?"

It was a brave but a rash thing to do as the Nips were always apprehensive of anyone approaching them and were likely to get very dangerous. The Korean guards, led by Kasiyama, most of them with sticks or clubs, rushed at Greg, knocked him down and started beating and kicking him. But he persisted, and went on shouting, "You say we have disobeyed orders. What orders?" Kasiyama could understand.

By this time Bamboo had got through the first two ranks. My rank was therefore in full view, and there was I facing him. He gave me one look, and the next thing I knew I was back again in the ranks. I said to my neighbour, "What happened to me? My hip hurts."

He said, "You got a corker. It came up from due south, and you went for a bender - flat. As you tried to rise he kicked you down again and stamped on your hip."

I could scarcely believe him as I remembered nothing, but my other neighbour then said, "Thank God I managed to stand up." I looked at him incredulously. "My dear fellow," I said, "you positively bit the dust."

He denied it and was very angry with me for suggesting it. And I realised that like him I too was suffering with what the medicos call post-concussive amnesia.

Bamboo got through twenty-seven out of thirty-five before his attention was drawn to the demands of Greg, who was now surrounded by guards. He repeated his demands and Kasiyama translated. To everybody's surprise Bamboo just stumped away putting on his coat and telling us to fall in again. As with Yoshida, the flame had burnt out.

We rejoined our comrades who had been watching this scene with every sympathy. But it was obvious that we were not entirely finished with Bamboo. He had regained the original loss of face and had saved Kasiyama's, but he still had to regain the face that he had lost by his temper with us. Sure enough, he came storming across the compound, making strange Nip noises, with Kasiyama close at his heels. He got on to a table out in front of the parade and let us have it in Japanese, a good ten minutes' worth, with Kasiyama translating snatches in the pauses or when told to do so.

We could not hear all he said in his squeaky voice, but as far as I can recall it was something to this effect: "You are prisoners of the Japanese. You must obey every Japanese order." (Old stuff and we were tired of it.) "We look after you very well. We give you three meals a day." (Murmurs of "What meals?") "We punish all men who do not behave. We are more 'croolie' than you." (He meant "cruel" to which we wholly agreed.) "You ought to know by now how we punish mistakes. The men from Haruku have told you about me. I will do the same here." And so on.

Then he finished and called over to him a wing commander named Maguire who was standing in front of us. It was a nervous moment as it was clear Maguire was going to catch it. He stopped in front of Bamboo, who was still standing on the table, and saluted. Bending down, Bamboo picked up a large wooden chair, a kind of garden chair. Raising it above his head he started to crash it down on Maguire's head, and a gasp of horror went up from every prisoner on parade. But as that great brute of a Nip swung it down, the whole chair, a rickety old thing that had been discarded for firewood, just came apart in his hands.

In a flash the tension that had been built up to a terrific climax was suddenly punctured with laughter. Bamboo was wild, but all he did was jump off the table and slam Maguire under the jaw. Maguire went flat, but got up again, very groggily, re-adjusted his side cap, saluted and came back towards us. He did it very well, though he was so dizzy he could not walk straight.

Bamboo turned away and strode off. It was the end of the scene from his point of view, and we did not see him again that night. It was now about 7.30 p.m., and his last orders were, "No supper for anyone and the British to remain fallen in opposite the guardhouse all night."

Having moved there we waited some time. After a while a sergeant, Bamboo's assistant, arrived and much parleying went on. He was informed that we did not understand what they wanted. Perhaps a misunderstanding had occurred, and as a show of good faith a few token volunteers were produced and a promise given to investigate the matter more fully in the morning. Then, after more face-saving and further parleying everyone was satisfied. The Nip fell us out and told the galley to serve supper to all the camp. It was then 10 p.m. - the whole business had lasted five hours.

In the circumstances, a parade of five hours interspersed with terror tactics, physical assault and no food since noon, should have taken a lot out of us. But we had gone through it without turning a hair. The only serious damage we had sustained was one broken jaw, but we had won a moral battle. It was a great scene, this - one of our proudest, and I can remember every detail as clearly as if it had happened yesterday, except of course for moments of post-concussive amnesia.

12

The Gate that Pop Never Built

Obviously the demand for technicians had come from Headquarters and heads would roll if it were not met. The result so far had been disappointing, so two days after the beat-up came an order demanding the names of all those who could drive, or knew anything about a motor car. This was a clever ruse to get some names, so to counter it we put down the names of all the British in the contingent. If they were crafty so were we; the game was beginning to intrigue us.

Their next move was to parade us and to cast the net again - for "experienced" drivers. We asked what "experienced" meant, and they said "able to drive for longer than ten years".

A number of people so qualified kept out, fearing that they would be employed on repair work or the like, but I joined this party. I reasoned that in the unlikely event of their allowing me, as an officer P.O.W., to drive a vehicle round Java, I could write it off in a week or so with ease and without suspicion. And if they employed me on repair work I could guarantee no car under my care would ever go as I knew nothing about cars.

About two hundred joined the "experienced" drivers. They then called for those with six years experience, then for those with three years experience. Those that still remained were young men who had never learned to drive and the liars who could but would not admit it. A number of these were invited to volunteer to learn to be "car-painters". As this was better than mixing cement or working on air-strips, it was well subscribed. The joke was that what they really wanted were carpenters.

The remainder were then further reduced by "those able to change a wheel" or "wheel changers," thus bringing the number of "technicians" on draft to 1,000, which seemed to please the Nips concerned. Presumably they had satisfied Headquarters. Next, the rumours started regarding our destination and duty.

Some said Nippon, others Singapore, but the best informed said Batavia, to re-open the General Motors assembly plant at Tangjong Priok, which proved correct. Bamboo said we would be away for only three months, after which we would return again. We were not particularly keen on being billeted in Tangjong Priok as malaria was very bad there; besides the place was likely to get a hammering from the air and sea before an assault, and the thought of being killed by your own side was particularly abhorrent to all P.O.W.s. It would have been too much - too much sheer poetic injustice in dying like that after all we had been through.

Within a fortnight we were off in two groups of five hundred, on consecutive days. I was in the second group, back again at the old familiar business of packing and farewells, with uncertainty as to our destination heightened by the dread of a journey to Nippon. Actually I did not mind so much this time as I detested the stone walls of the L.O.G. with its nauseous overcrowding. I felt anything was better than that. Most of the Navy were on this draft, but we had arranged for a really competent lieutenant, Hutcheson, to stay and look after the sailors.

The day we left was July 5th, 1945, and the 120 miles to Batavia took us twenty-five hours. We fell in at 10 a.m. to be counted and searched. This took over two hours in the hot sun. At 12.30 we got a good meal of rice, served and eaten in the parade compound; as this adjoined the barrack compounds it was simple enough to collect contraband which had been left behind. We were given a small loaf of tapioca bread and two bananas as rations for the trip.

At 1.30 we fell in again. Kasiyama had got some lorries for us, and these were to be filled with the heavy packs belonging to "weak men, old men, senior officers and junior officers," in that order. Most people however got something taken for them; and just as well as we had a long march ahead of us. The group the day before had only just managed to make the station; which was why Kasiyama had produced the lorries for us.

At 2 p.m. we set off. We had already spent four hours standing about in the sun, and those four miles to the station at Bandoeng at true midday (Nip time was two hours ahead of the local time) along scorching roads remains one of the hottest experiences I can recall. We were all quite weak with exhaustion and parched with thirst when we reached the station.

Kasiyama really excelled himself on this occasion - there was a great drum of tea waiting for us, another lesson learned from the sufferings of the pioneer group the day before.

It was now about four o'clock. We piled into five third class coaches, in which we remained, a mass of sweating humanity, for another three hours.

We were packed so close together that for us to number consecutively became a problem which we made insurmountable to complicate matters for the guards. We tried first in Japanese, then in Dutch, then in English, and got a different answer each time - 91, 89, and 95. Our Nip guard was very worried as he was responsible for the safe custody of all in his coach. We knew the answer was 92 - just how I do not remember, but when we told him he did not believe us. He gave up the unequal struggle in the end.

After a lot of aimless shunting we finally started at 7 p.m. for Batavia. As we were attached to a goods train, there were further interludes for shunting at every biggish station down the line, and it took nine hours to get to Mangerei, on the outskirts of Batavia. At this junction, the train stopped for two hours till dawn had broken. It was very cold in the early morning and we were tired and hungry.

At last, at 8 a.m., we pulled into one of the minor stations in Batavia, after sixteen hours in the train and altogether twenty-two hours since we had fallen in at Bandoeng. Little Colonel Kawabe was on the platform to meet us - not an inspiring sight at that or any stage of the journey. Then, after falling in and mustering again, we marched through the suburbs of Batavia for a mile and a half to the Cycle Camp - a welcome sight (after L.O.G.) with the British C.O. there to greet us and many old faces about. The camp was clean and spacious, and after being enclosed by high stone walls, it was reassuring to be able to look out at the houses and gardens of the suburb of Kramat. Moreover, everything seemed peaceful, without tension.

After a further two hours to have our gear searched, we finally flopped down into our billets at 11 a.m. with a cup of tea. After that we shaved and doused ourselves with water, unlimited water, in a bath house - sheer heaven after L.O.G. where we washed in the open or in a tiny room with hordes of others milling round.

I was in a room near my old billet in Barrack 7, with Ramsay-Rae, a wing commander, an Australian and a splendid fellow, who became boss of the "drivers and carpainters". For a fortnight nothing happened. All 1,000 of us did nothing at all. It was a lovely existence, relaxed, being able to spread ourselves, the food reasonable by prison camp standards, the guards quiet, and the Japanese Commandant fairly ineffectual.

We could now see for ourselves the truth behind the rumours that the Nips were cracking up. We found the guards mixed up in black market rackets with the P.O.W.s, bringing in forbidden food which they sold at a high profit to our chief racketeers, who re-sold it to other prisoners at an even higher profit. Thus an egg cost 7s. 6d. in the equivalent of Japanese paper which was rapidly losing value.

Inevitably the guards were far more lax than before. The sergeant was still the same - Nakamura, who had once been rather strict as Soni's right hand man but not too bad a fellow though brainless. Now he seemed apathetic. There were obsequious Koreans putting in a good word for themselves with certain officers, whom they came to see about "The future of Korea after the war and the possibilities of friendship between our country and the Western Powers". They tried to make out that they hated the Nips but had been forced by them to go along the same path. We were not impressed. If the Nips had been winning it would have been an entirely different tune. These Koreans had been very nasty to us and we could not forget it.

At last the car party started work. The technicians, "carpainters," wheel changers and some of the drivers as administrators, were formed into a working party. They had to go to Tangjong Priok, leaving the camp daily at 6 a.m. A special train took them from Batavia to the port, where they worked in the General Motors assembly plant. They worked a long day, with only an hour off for dinner at noon and a short break in the afternoon, repairing Japanese transport and converting saloon cars into light troop carriers. The latter entailed cutting off the body abaft the driver's seat with hammer and chisel and fitting on wooden seats for eight men. Some shining new Packards were among the cars to be thus modified, and though it seemed a shameful waste of good cars, the P.O.W.s quite enjoyed doing it as it meant a dead loss to the Nips.

The "technically efficient" were given a fortnight to learn how milling and other machines worked, and by claiming ignorance and inexperience, were able to excuse themselves for the considerable damage done to machines and tools. Those not "technically efficient" were employed on repairing broken down cars and trucks under a Welsh gunner captain, G. Ashe. They turned it into a great game.

Any car which could not go had its engine stripped completely; every nut and bolt, every spring and moving part was taken out, cleaned, polished and laid out on the floor. The bits were then systematically put together again and the car sent on to trained Chinese mechanics who were on the permanent staff there. If the car worked the Chinese said it was unsatisfactory and turned it down. This meant it was completely re-stripped and put together again, and a whole week would thus be wasted. If the car was defective the Chinese adjusted it so that it would run for a few days and passed it as satisfactory. And it would be back again within a week for another crazy refit.

At the end of the first working week five cars had been repaired. The number rose to eight in the second week, but of these four were from the first week's output back for refit. Still the Nips appeared delighted with the whole set-up, and we learned that the Bandoeng camp staff got the credit for having sent such a good P.O.W. party. The Batavia staff also got a pat on the back for organising such an efficient car repair and truck manufacturing scheme, and the local Nips in charge were congratulated on their output. Even the P.O.W.s were told that they were working very well. It was a veritable jamboree of face-saving and mutual and self admiration that completely obscured the true state of affairs. Typically Japanese, it reminds me of another of their bureaucratic absurdities. We would invariably receive a warning by way of a hint from a guard whenever the Kempetai were planning a surprise check on the camp, so that secret wireless sets and other forbidden possessions would immediately go underground. The Kempetai would search but find nothing incriminating - and the guards would be praised for running a trouble free camp. On the other hand the guards would have lost face and got into trouble had the surprise check uncovered any of our illegal operations. There was never any question of the guards and the Kempetai working together. It was apparently so much simpler the other way.

At times the Japanese seemed possessed of a gargantuan stupidity - they seemed incapable of grasping the simple and the obvious. Once the Kempetai found six rounds of pistol ammunition in an Australian's kit and there was consternation among the guards. Vicious looking Kempetai detectives gouged through every nook and cranny in the barrack room, tearing mattresses apart and throwing kit all over the place in a vain search for the pistol. The Australian said he had surrendered it on capitulation three years before but had just kept the rounds in the bottom of his knapsack where they had remained and somehow been overlooked in the many searches when changing camps. They threw him into the cells for a time and interrogated him pretty severely, but he stuck to his story and eventually they preferred to forget the whole thing, and sent him back to camp. In fact, the pistol was sewn into the back of his belt, which was lying on the ground in front of them.

At first the "experienced car-drivers" were not employed. We were to wait until production had increased, when we would be put on driving convoys of converted cars as they came off the production line from the works to Batavia. So we sat in the camp and did nothing.

To keep myself occupied, I worked in the vegetable garden which was over the road from the camp and ran down to a canal. I thought gardening might be fun since the Nips were quiet and were leaving us alone, but the weather was very hot and dry at that time and the plants wanted a lot of water. This meant carting it in buckets from the canal. I got rather bored with this form of sport, so I retired from this party and took over a party of fifty officers who were being sent out daily to work at a school about three miles away. Being the senior one, I became the "*hunsho*" or leader, which was the job to have as the "*hunsho*" merely organised the others and the Nips considered that he was excused from labour.

The party was composed of all services and all types and on the whole were a good crowd of fellows. We were employed on building a guardhouse and ceremonial gateway to a school, which was to be used as a depot for the Heihos, a semi-military organisation of conscripted Javanese youths under Japanese command. The work involved brick-laying and concrete mixing, concerning both of which we all pleaded complete ignorance.

The Nip in charge, a very pleasant little man with glasses whom we called Pop, was very keen on his gateway and guardhouse and, what was more, knew exactly how to build them. He had a good sense of humour, was tactful, appreciated that we were officers, and rarely got angry or hit anyone. He laid the bricks himself and told us how to mix the concrete. The proportions of sand, water and cement he varied according to the work in hand, whether the surface concerned was vertical or horizontal and for various reasons of his own.

Sometimes he would say one water, one sand, two cement. So we would mix two water, two sand, and one cement. Then he might change it to one water, two sand, one cement and we would mix two water, one sand, two cement. Sometimes he got suspicious, in which case we would mix them correctly until he turned away, when in went another spadeful of one of the ingredients. Poor Pop. It was inevitable that his gate would collapse when the monsoon rains started. But he was never to know that disappointment.

We had been on the job for about two and a half weeks and were still doing it on August 14th, 1945. That evening we came back to camp as usual and were prepared to go out again the next morning. We had heard on the ice-box about the atom bomb on Hiroshima, but none of us quite understood what it meant; oddly enough, when we did, although we hated the Nips and considered no punishment too severe for them, we were quite shocked at the thought of such an atom bomb being dropped on a town. We just could not understand why its terrible power had not been first shown to the Japanese, by dropping it on a plain or on a mountain. That, at any rate, was the way most British P.O.W.s felt about it at the time.

The car party were very late that night. The trains were disorganised, and they reported strange goings on in the factory. They said that the Chinese thought that the war was ending, and that the Nips were already selling the lathes and tools. But this sort of rumour we had heard for years and little notice was taken. That night we all turned in as we normally did, all prepared to go out next morning to our various jobs. But this was not to be. History would intervene and Pop's ceremonial gate would never be completed.

13

The Ice-box Closes Down

On the night of August 14th I slept as usual in a room with the British S.O. and his adjutant, at the end of a barrack which accommodated about three hundred British soldiers and airmen. It was a quiet night, but at about 5 a.m. there was the sound of Japanese guards running about and shouting, followed by face-slapping. Some of the Dutch were involved; they had gone into the bathroom before reveillé to get a wash before the rush started. They were always doing this and causing trouble, and it was nothing of particular interest. The adjutant went out to have a look, and soon came back saying, "It's only the Gottverdommers. None of our men mixed up in it. But they have closed all the gates and there are guards everywhere."

We thought this was probably due to an air raid warning, or possibly news of an assault convoy at sea in the vicinity. It was not unusual, a panic of this sort. So we went to sleep again.

Reveillé went at 7.00 and everything seemed pretty normal. But at 7.20 a messenger arrived from the guardhouse to say that there would be no muster at 7.30 and that everyone was to remain in the barracks. This was indeed something, and rumours started to race around the camp - that air reconnaissance planes were taking photographs and the Nips were intent on hiding us, that an invasion had started, that the war was over, and so on. The Nips had never missed a muster before, and it was indeed a red letter day.

At 8.00, they sent along to say that no working parties would go out. I was sure there must be something momentous behind it, but I could get nothing out of the ice-box source. The officer who ran one of them knew nothing, or rather he started playing the bluff that he thought the war was over. Actually he knew it was over but, with the few others who had got the latest ice-cream, had agreed to keep it quiet. They feared that if we got the news before the Nips had given it to us it might have been used as an excuse by our captors to liquidate us. The first news of the Italian surrender in 1943 had been given to the guards at Bandoeng by the P.O.W.s and there had been a frightful stink about it by the Nips.

I was sure the ice-cream vendor was bluffing, I knew him well enough. Besides I knew that on certain occasions I was meant to suspect the vendors, then to keep quiet and play the same game. Anyhow, the camp morale went soaring, the air filled with optimistic conjecture, while the guards remained uncommunicative, sullen and quiet. The weather was hot and sunny but pleasant.

Next day the routine was the same. There were no musters, no work. Now it was quite obvious that the war was over, and the Nip guards had begun saying so quite openly. We heard things like "War finished", "Now we all friends", "Now we all go home", to which there were guarded but appropriate replies. Their malice and sadism were not going to be forgotten. The Japanese doctor came into the camp and showered us with M. and B.[1] and other drugs which had been denied us all these years.

Curiously there was no wild jubilation now that the war was at last over. We had been through a Japanese hell, and we had survived. We took it as it came. There were even some qualms about the final liberation with the inevitable snapping of ties of great friendship and uncertainty about the future which we would now have to face. We had become institutionalised and apathetic through our imprisonment, and our poor state of health had sapped our vitality. For years, while death had stood round the corner, we had accepted the good with the bad without much emotion. We had lost our capacity for excessive joy or excitement, which was why there were no victory scenes.

Day followed day with the Nips producing all sorts of things out of their hat. First there was soap, not one cake but six for each man. Then came an ingratiating succession of shorts, shirts, socks, blankets, nearly all of Nippon manufacture, but no official declaration of peace. The B.B.C. had not yet confirmed that all the enemy forces had agreed

---

[1]May and Baker antibiotic tablets

to capitulate; in fact it had been hinted that opposition might continue in outlying places, and we were not certain whether this was only an armistice or a peace. It was against the Nips creed to announce a defeat; the word was not in their military vocabulary. In their news bulletins they had never admitted even the loss of an aircraft. They would merely say that so many aircraft had not yet returned or had self-blasted themselves into their objectives.

As for the guards, they were pleasant and subdued, and their officers were little in evidence. Though the Nips did not show it, undoubtedly they all felt defeat very much, and, oddly enough their stoical impassiveness made the situation almost an embarrassment to us. We knew that they were going to have to pay for what they had done to us; their future was hopeless.

Their local administration had started to break down. Transport was not available, the native drivers having left, so that it was soon necessary to provide truck drivers to take out lorries under their orders to maintain supplies both to P.O.W. and civilian camps. Of course, such jobs were a wonderful change and great fun for the soldiers and airmen who were given them. Rackets and black market transactions flourished apace, and some of the wilder spirits broke out of camp and took French leave in the town although this was greatly discouraged and kept down to a minimum only by threat of severe disciplinary action involving delayed evacuation till everyone had gone.

There were several good reasons for this. The Japanese were still in charge, and we did not wish to aggravate them now. We knew they had been made responsible for our safety and well-being by Mountbatten, and did not want to give them an excuse if anything went wrong. Besides we were never quite certain which way they might turn. A local commander, suicidally inclined, might say, "The future has nothing for me. The British will probably condemn me to death for maltreatment of prisoners, so I will take all these prisoners with me." In addition, Javanese nationalist elements, organised by the Nips, were determined to resist the return of the Dutch, and there was no knowing how that situation might develop. Personally, I think of the period between August 15th 1945 and our final departure from the East Indies

The author with draft of naval prisoners-of-war which arrived at Batavia from Macassar in August 1945

as one of the most dangerous of the whole period of captivity.

A fortnight before, a draft of three hundred had arrived from Macassar and had immediately been isolated in a barrack which was wired off and screened with a high atap fence. Among these were David Chubb, Mark Kerr and three other naval officers with thirty-nine ratings from the British naval contingent. They were not particularly well, but quite passable compared with some of the small island drafts which normally came into this camp. But their news was very bad.

By the time I had left in October 1943, twenty-three men had died. The number was now 183 with three more so ill as certain to die. Doc Wyatt had always said the third year would be the worst. There had been dysentery epidemics in early 1945 in which some 100 men had died. But there was no doubt about it that this tragically high number of fatalities was due almost entirely to the diabolical tyranny of Yoshida, who had got much worse after the bulk of officers had left.

David had the list with him, and it was sad to read it, page after page of names of good men and old friends. A later study of the list confirmed several observations I had already made concerning the relationship between the age of the prisoner and his ability to survive sickness. The first of these was that those in the thirties were the best equipped with the mental and physical stamina required for the ordeal of prolonged hardship. There were twenty-nine deaths in this group. The remainder were in the twenties, when a man lacks true mental stamina, and in the older age groups when a physical decline has set in. Only one of a dozen chief stokers had survived. But the highest death rate had been among the red heads - all thirteen had died.

David reported that the rest of the people left at Macassar were in an awful state - nearly all with beri-beri and malaria. He did not know what would happen, but thought that Yoshida had a scheme to march all who could walk into the hills and that that would mean many more casualties. There had been "death marches" of a similar sort in Tarakan in Borneo and in the Philippines, and it was obvious that early assistance would be required if we were to get the surviving sailors safely out of the clutches of this maniac. Meanwhile, however, there was nothing we could do but wait for our liberators to come.

All the P.O.W.s left at Bandoeng came down to join us on the week-end of August 26th, and it was good to see them again. The problem now was keeping something like 3,000 P.O.W.s under control; there was always the fear that a lynching party (and there were some very obstreperous Dutch) might kick over the traces and string up a few Nips on a tree. Then anything might happen. Also, it was quite possible that extremist elements among the Indonesians might break into the camp and kidnap or murder Dutchmen.

As a precaution, we secretly organised security platoons. I had one of these composed of officers who slept in the vicinity of my billet. We were told to be ready at a moment's notice, especially at night, and I told my lot to wear something white above the waist, a white shirt or sash, as a distinguishing mark. Each was also to have a cudgel of some kind immediately to hand, but one which could be left about without attracting much attention.

Very soon every one got impatient. The P.O.W. expects immediate attention. He thinks he is deserving of the topmost priority, and that the resources of the nation should be geared to liberating him as soon as possible, sweeping all other considerations aside. He did not stop to think of the great ocean distances involved, that minefields would have to be swept, shipping diverted from the offensive to the rescue, fuel replenishment arranged, or that our high command might not even know where we were, as indeed they did not.

A general estimate was a fortnight for rescue to come, but the more astute said October and they were not far wrong. Men got very restless, and somewhat undisciplined as they knew now that the Nips would not punish them and that it would be difficult for us to do so. A lot of the Dutch went out of camp to look for their wives and children. It was hard to stop them, but fortunately most of them were sensible about it and were restrained by the moderate advice given them.

Instructions were received from the Supreme Allied Commander to paint P.O.W. in white letters across camps, and to mark suitable runways on fields. We did all this with relish. But nothing came near us, not an aircraft, not a ship, not even a wireless message for over a fortnight. Though life was easy the food was poor. We had asked for more, but nothing had been done; besides the Japanese had still not informed us officially that the war was over.

Eventually, Wing Commander Ramsay-Rae, the S.O. of the camp, went to them and asked for some official declaration. The Nips reacted quickly to this request; they were in fact waiting for it, but hoped, I think, that we would not make it. The Camp Commandant gave orders that all senior officers would be required to fall in at 10 p.m. - a funny time, we thought, and there was much conjecture about what was going to happen.

I was considerably excited at the prospect, and was glad I was to be one of the party. This was going to be one of those moments in a lifetime you never forget - one for which we had waited and lived for three and a half years - the moment when these little yellow devils would have to admit to us that they had lost the war.

I put on my best clothes, things I had carefully preserved for just this occasion. I was the Senior Naval Officer and therefore representing my service. It was not exactly a smart turn-out, but exceptional compared with our usual rags. I wore white tropical shorts and a shirt, neither of which were patched, while my shoulder straps were the very ones I had been wearing when my ship was sunk and which I had worn continuously throughout captivity. Sewn into these straps were certain documents which no Nip had found in any search, and which included a copy of the money loan agreement with the Dutch, and our casualty lists. My hat was camp made. I had no stockings, but white ankle socks and black shoes.

The pipe-down went precisely at ten. Perhaps that was the idea - to get the camp turned in and quiet before this business. Or perhaps they thought there might be a cheering mob and possibly trouble. We had gone along at 9.45 and fallen in outside the Nip office, the place still redolent of Soni and others, of beat-ups, of drafts being picked, of searches. It stank of evil practices, of doubts and fears and acute physical discomfort.

After a short interval one of the Nip guards came out and told us to fall out. He explained that there would be some delay and that we were to sit and rest on the grass slopes of the rose garden which was in the rear of the square. He produced several packets of Kooas - a local made Nip cigarette, at that time the height of smoking luxury. So we sat, smoked, and waited. Time drew on and still nothing happened. It was a warm starry night, and a few hours in three and a half years did not worry us much.

Activity commenced at five minutes to midnight, when the Camp Commandant arrived and we were told to fall in. It was intimated that the correct and normal marks of respect were expected to be paid when Japanese senior officers arrived. We had for so long been giving salutes to Nips, down to the most junior soldier, that a few more, and a call to attention meant nothing to us. In any case, they still held the power.

Nakamura, the sergeant, was putting up a kind of dais. It was rather pathetic and so typically Japanese; everything was done on the cheap, and here too was a miserable affair of milk boxes and planks to push his boss a little higher in the air than we were.

Just before midnight big arc lights came on and Colonel Kawabe arrived, still the little rat we knew, with his shirt collar outside his coat lapels and no tie. He was a wizened little man of about five feet and I should say well over sixty; and he had been getting much thinner and older looking in the past year much to our delight. No one had a good word for Kawabe. Though we hated the bashers, many had some good qualities and had at one time or another been helpful or kind. Kawabe had never done anything for any P.O.W. He was evil and mean right through. He had control of all camps in the Batavia area, and whenever he came around there was trouble. He was continually reducing the food, but would hypocritically bow and place wreaths on the graves of those who died by his malice and neglect.

We were called to attention and reported. The Camp Commandant stood on one side of the dais, Nakamura and a Malay interpreter on the other, and some guards went behind. Kawabe mounted the dais. Under the bright lights his face looked a very pale greyish yellow. In his jack-boots and floppy uniform, with a big sword at his side and a paper in his hand, he looked like a grotesque ventriloquist's doll perched rather precariously on the milk-box dais. We looked at him straight in the face, waiting for his announcement, but he spoke in Japanese, of which none of us understood a word. It seemed to take some time.

At the end of his speech, Kawabe handed a copy of what he had said to the Malay interpreter and told him to read it to us, but the copy was apparently in English and the interpreter could not read it. Kawabe had brought either the wrong copy or the wrong interpreter. However the Camp Commandant could speak English, and he was given permission to translate it for us. It was from Kawabe's superior, a general; and it was to this effect:

> To all Prisoners and Internees.
>
> I have been ordered to inform you that there has been a cessation of arms. The hardships of a prisoner-of-war life during more than three and a half years must have been strenuous, and I must express my respects to you on account of that. After three years I have administered to you in the best way possible and with my best staff, but during war it is not always possible to give all that is necessary.
>
> I understand that you have had hardships and had to live in small camps with limited food. I have tried to look after your health. Until my administration ceases and you take charge, I want you to carry on as before. I want you to look after your health. Let the behaviour as it has been up to now remain until our administration has ceased. I hope there will be no mistakes.
>
> I pray for your health and happiness in the future.
>
> TAKADO.
>
> *Chief of Java Prisoner-of-War and Internee Camps.*

Some Royal Navy and Royal Marine officers in the Cycle Camp Batavia after the Japanese capitulation

It was an amazing declaration - no mention of defeat, only a cessation of arms, and that the administration was going to change, with the ominous hope at the end of it that there would be no "mistakes". They still had the guns.

Ramsay-Rae immediately stepped forward. "Can I be provided with a copy of this declaration, please?" he asked Kawabe.

"I am very sorry but this is the only copy I have," was the reply he received. "I see," said Ramsay Rae. "Anyway, thank you for the announcement," he went on. "I would like to congratulate the Camp Commandant on the excellent way he read it in English."

This gave the Camp Commandant considerable "face" over Kawabe, who was keen to conclude the painful episode and had now got down from his rickety dais and was moving towards the gate.

"Just a moment please," Ramsay-Rae called after him. "I have some questions which I want you to answer."

"I am very busy," Kawabe whined. "I am in charge of all the camps in Batavia and have a lot of work to do."

"But I have some vital demands to make, and as Commander of all the Batavia camps you should listen to me."

Kawabe went very pale and looked distinctly embarrassed. "Any requests should be made in the morning to the Camp Commandant," he said. "I give orders that he must attend to them."

"All right, I will hold you to that."

Kawabe left. We never saw him again.

We fell out and returned to our barracks. A number of officers were waiting to hear the news, but there was not much to tell them. Back in our room we had a conference about it. For some reason the R.A.F. did not want to do anything about it that night, but the Navy were adamant that we should make an announcement to all British P.O.W.s at the morning parade at 9 a.m., which meant that we had to stay up and reconstruct the declaration. Harkness, our Paymaster, suggested that each of us should try to remember one sentence or phrase, which we did, and after a terrific effort pieced it together, as we believed, almost exactly. It took us till after 3 a.m. before we finished, and the Adjutant went off to type it for the morning parade. I have that copy still.

One of the things demanded of the Nips next day was a wireless set so that we could listen officially to the news. This they provided and bulletins were taken down by shorthand writers and copies circulated to all barracks. The icebox could now close down.

14

The Women of Tjideng

A squadron of Dutch Liberator bombers came early in September, flying very low over the camp. It was a stirring moment. Men climbed on to barrack roofs, waving and cheering, and the aircraft crew were hanging out of their entrance doors and cockpits. Then we got information that a repatriation team would be parachuted on to Batavia airfield.

We saw their Liberator come over and some of the parachutes drop. The party included an S.A.S.[2] major, an R.A.M.C. captain, a medical orderly and a wireless operator, with several canisters of medical stores. These men went into the various camps right through Java, and they did not waste much time. I had a few minutes with the doctor, who gave me some of the news; but we wanted to know so much it was difficult to know where to start. Even the parachutists' wings were new to us; so were their red berets, and a doctor parachutist was quite beyond our imagination. But what came as the biggest surprise to us was that till only recently the Allies had practically no knowledge of the Far Eastern P.O.W. camps or of the prisoners in them.

One day a squadron leader was dropped to reconnoitre the airfield to see whether it could cope with four engined aircraft. A working party from the camp went out to help get it into shape, the Nips having neglected it for years. Then some of the R.A.F. prisoners, officers and men, went out to take over the control of the airfield.

On September 8th our S.O. sent for me and asked if I would do a job in the women internees' camp at Tjideng. Apparently, Mountbatten wanted lists of all prisoners and internees quickly and the women at Tjideng were too worn out to cope with all the typing. He was sending ten army and R.A.F. clerks up to the camp, and as there were

---

[2]Special Air Service

some 10,000 women and children in this camp he thought that an officer should go in charge, and a senior officer at that. I said I would go willingly. I was keen to get out of the camp and do something useful and different for a change.

We drove out to Tjideng at dusk and were met by the Camp Commandant, a long, lanky Nip captain called Saki, who received me courteously. The senior Dutch typist was there too. Luckily she spoke English very well, so could explain to me exactly what was required. The men would work in the guardhouse, which was a large bungalow, in a room off that of the Nip Commandant and his staff. The lists were to be ready in three days - fifteen copies of 10,000 names with each person's address, age, sex and name and address of next of kin - a herculean task that was simplified in no way for us by some of the Dutch names. Nationalities had also to be separated, and the lists we had to work from were well thumbed camp lists with those who had died crudely crossed off.

There were only about 130 British women in this camp, including some Australians and New Zealanders, mostly missionaries and social welfare workers. The senior of these was a Miss Nicolich from Singapore, very capable and extremely charming, who had her aged mother in the camp with her. She immediately set about arranging accommodation, bedding and food for our men, whom I decided should stay between the two wires of the camp. Most Nip camps were contained within an inner barrier beyond which was a gap in which the guardhouse was always situated, the whole being enclosed within an outer barrier. In this gap at Tjideng there were several empty bungalows adjoining the guardhouse. One of these was put at my disposal, and the next two given to my men. Several young Dutch girls volunteered to look after us, and they produced, goodness knows from where, some mattresses and cooking utensils and set up house for us. I tried to refuse these articles, as I said I was sure the women could not spare them, but my objections were swept aside.

"Your men have got a big job to do and they must get proper rest when they are off duty," was Miss Nicolich's last word on the subject.

Some rice and fruit were produced for the men for supper, and I said we would start at 8 p.m. and work all night, stopping only when men dropped over the keys. They started willingly, but took some time to get the hang of the lists. When there were queries, I sent for the senior Dutch typist and she sorted them out. In fact, she stayed around to help and was very efficient. She had an intense loathing for the Nips and Saki, whom she stood up to and ticked off whenever he interfered. I admired her courage.

The ladies decided that I must have someone to do my house and bring me my food, and they selected a fair-haired Dutch girl called Lily to do the job. Lily was great fun, aged about nineteen, fluent in English and full of life. She said she was engaged and that her fiancé was in one of the Bandoeng camps, or at least she hoped he was; none of these women knew for sure where their menfolk were. Lily used to scrounge all sorts of things for my party and me - eggs, mangoes, bananas, coffee. She could cook anything, and conjured up some splendid alfresco dishes it seemed out of nothing.

We worked nearly all that first night, the men typing in relays while I checked and sorted the finished pages. The men wanted to pack up at two o'clock, but I said no. I organised regular breaks and brewed some tea which had been thoughtfully left for us. By 4.30 men were starting to drop over the keys, so I sent everyone to bed with orders to be back at nine.

Next day I altered the routine to three 4-hour periods with a meal in between. But by 8 p.m. they were pretty tired, and I packed up at 9 p.m. We had broken the back of it, and were able to finish the rest of the job next day, to the great relief of Saki and his minions who were terrified that they were going to get into trouble for being late. The lists left on September 11th, in a white painted aircraft for Saigon. It was a good bit of work - fifteen copies of the particulars of 10,000 people - and the men, none of whom was exactly fit, were pretty tired at the end of it.

Saki reported our efforts to our Camp Commandant, who came up to see us. I was asked into the guard room and profusely thanked and congratulated by him. It was their job to keep proper records and to provide them on demand by the Supreme Allied Commander. We had done it for them and saved their face, and he went back to the Cycle Camp and gave me a splendid write-up to the British S.O.

While my party had been busy typing I had gone round the Tjideng camp - an eerie experience seeing thousands and thousands of women and except for an odd guard or two, not a male adult anywhere. There were children dressed only in shorts or bathing slips, rushing round in hordes like tribes of pigmies. The boys were all under twelve. Once they reached that age they used to be taken from their mothers and put in a boys' camp.

I heard later the death roll had been very heavy, especially among the older women after the move here from inland camps in January 1945, travelling under conditions similar to those we had experienced. While I was at Tjideng - ten days - between three and five people went out dead every day. What shocked me particularly was the callousness of the young girls at the sight of so much death among them. I remember once, as the hearse went out, hearing Lily casually remark, "I wonder who's that going out in the box there?"

"Lily," I said. "You should not speak like that."

"Why?" she asked in all innocence. "What have I said wrong?"

There was evidence of Soni's handiwork. Senior women, all street and block commanders, were wearing bandeaus over their heads which had been shaved by his orders. Yet despite their privations, grief and sufferings, the morale of all these women was wonderful. All those I saw were spotlessly clean, beautifully turned out, cheerful and in great spirits. They had stood up to the Nips and I have nothing but admiration for the courage and determination for those Dutch women in adversity.

They ran the whole camp themselves. A Miss Roda was the boss, a quiet, dignified, elderly lady. She, alone among those concerned in the administration, had not been subjected to the hair deprivation punishment by Soni. She had just refused and even Soni had not dared. Women and girls did all the camp chores - the cooking and food distribution, the cleaning even of the sewers and drains, wood chopping, repairs and a host of other things besides. I saw Dutch girls unloading large bags of rice off a lorry with great fervour, a feat which I doubt I could have tackled myself at the time.

The camp had been formed by enclosing three streets of modern bungalows with barbed wire and atap, the whole area about twenty acres. Though on the outside the place was alive and cheerful looking, inside the houses it was a vastly different story. I had thought, when we were in the L.O.G., that we were pretty tightly packed. But that was luxury compared with the way in which these women lived. The bungalows, built generally for four people, now accommodated over fifty in some cases. Women were huddled in small groups in the corners of the stuffy rooms, some brewing tea, others cooking - the camp galleys only cooked the rice and some of the vegetables. The sick and old seemed everywhere, and the squalor from overcrowding was too frightful to describe.

As elsewhere in conquered territories, here too the Japanese military discipline had safeguarded women and children from sexual assault. Any guard reported for getting fresh was beaten up by his commander and removed.

I hope I shall never see another Tjideng, yet for all its horror, I have a pleasant memory of the place. It was a change from the routine of prison life. After the typing was done, some of us stayed on to help with odd jobs. I was asked to act as a liaison officer between Tjideng and the Cycle Camp, to organise some help from the P.O.W.s to relieve the girls of the tougher manual jobs. I soon had working parties of fifty to a hundred men coming up daily. Naturally these parties were oversubscribed by the Dutchmen in the Cycle Camp, as many had wives, families or girl friends at Tjideng, but I found no work being done. Eventually I arranged for the Cycle Camp to send half Dutch and half British. The British came to work and did so happily, while the Dutch I regarded only as visitors.

I also arranged for a number of the sick to be sent down to the Hotel des Indes, now a repatriation centre, and for mothers and daughters living in separate camps to be brought together; there were a lot of girls in a camp near the Cycle Camp at Kramat.

One of our problems at the time was to stop women and girls breaking out of the camp at night. There were armed bands of Indonesian hooligans roving round the Tjideng camp, throwing stones over the perimeter and generally being nasty. The Nips had increased their guards, and it was nothing to hear shots fired in the night. The Indonesian revolution against the Dutch was already starting - as I discovered for myself one evening when I had to go down to the Hotel des Indes to arrange early repatriation for three English women, one of whom weighed only 63lb.

I had borrowed a car and took Miss Nicolich with me as I felt she was in need of an outing. An R.A.F. acquaintance of mine was running the show at the hotel and he gave us a real slap-up dinner.

After the meal we went for a drive. A bright moon was up, and the lush countryside was really beautiful. But just a few miles outside the city we found the road barred by a band of Indonesians armed with knives and sabres. We stopped and one of them came up on my side of the car. He asked me in Dutch who we were and where we were going.

I had learnt Dutch and understood exactly what he said. Normally, I would have replied in Dutch, but my sense of danger warned me not to do so. Instead I said in Malay, "I do not understand Dutch. I am English."

At that they at once allowed us to pass, but I feel certain that had I spoken in Dutch to those terrorists we should have been murdered on the spot. We wasted no time in returning to Batavia. Later on, many Dutch P.O.W.s who went out from the Cycle Camp were in fact ambushed and cut to pieces.

We returned to Tjideng to find the camp in an uproar, the place bristling with Nips with rifles and fixed bayonets. Apparently some Indonesian bands had got very threatening outside the camp, and some P.O.W.s, who had been sent up from the Cycle Camp as extra sentries, had got scared. A call had gone out to the Nips for help and in no time a full company of infantry had arrived in trucks. However, everything soon quietened down and we had no further trouble.

The saddest part of Tjideng is, I think, the fact that it remained occupied by Dutch women and children for another whole year. There was not the shipping available to take them back to Europe, and the situation in Java while they waited was too dangerous to risk letting them live unprotected and ordinary private lives.

There were some touching reunion scenes in the camp while I was there, when husbands came in and found their wives and children whom they had not seen for nearly four years. Generally the fathers found their children pretty fit - the women had given them most of the food - but they seemed to have made very little physical progress in captivity. I was always wrong about their ages - out by four years. Those I thought to be five or six were usually nine or ten.

While I was at Tjideng a number of New Zealand, American, Canadian and Australian aircraft flew in and lifted their nationals. The women and very sick went first. Some of the incoming pilots and air crews were rather obstreperous and off-hand with the Nips, which I did not like as the latter were still responsible for our safety. I had to speak very strongly to some New Zealanders in Tjideng who treated Saki with lack of courtesy and good manners.

"Don't think I'm Nip happy," I told them. "I shan't forget Tjideng as long as I live. But any behaviour likely to compromise the safety of these women and children cannot be tolerated."

15

"Grey Funnel"

The first P.O.W.s to be liberated from the Cycle Camp were the New Zealanders. Their aircraft were the first in and out of Batavia, taking the bulk of their personnel in one lift. And most of the rest of us were delighted they beat the Americans who had been somewhat over-confident that their planes would be first.

The Americans went next, then the Australians, then the Canadians. That left the Dutch and ourselves whose numbers were rather too large for evacuation by air.

For a long time now we had listened to the jibes of the Dutch who always blamed us for the loss of Malaya, Singapore and therefore the Far East. Their great heroes were the Americans who, we were told every day, would be the ones to rescue us. I was however prepared to wager against this. I told the sailors from the start that the White Ensign would come and fetch us, and that we would go out "grey funnel".

And sure enough, on September 12th, 1945, came word that H.M.S. *Cumberland* had left Colombo for Singapore and Java. This was just the news we wanted, and we were not slow to ram it down the throats of those who had supported the American rescue theory. Now their smile was on the other side of the face, and the Royal Navy suddenly became very popular.

It was arranged that four senior officers should go to Tandjong Priok to meet the ship when she arrived, and I was to be one of them. The difficulty was finding out when she was due and when she had actually arrived. She had ordered the Nips to meet her beyond Edam Island with charts of the minefields and assurances that the channels were safe. No one seemed to know whether she would anchor off or come into the port.

When she did arrive she was a day late and the negotiations with the Japanese High Command took some time. We set off about dusk dressed in our best outfits, though the effect, set off by our home-made caps, was bizarre to say the least.

As we drove into Priok docks the view of *Cumberland* anchored off was a memorable sight. There she was all lit up - her scuttle and upper deck lights full on - a view we had not seen anywhere since 1939. It was suddenly like the old days, and being ex-*Exeter* and therefore endeared to the 8-inch cruiser, we were glad a "County" had come. She was wearing the flag of Rear-Admiral W.R. Patterson, Flag Officer Commanding the 5th Cruiser Squadron, and commanded by Captain P.K. Enright. We had heard this over the wireless, but beyond these two officers we had no idea who any of the other officers might be.

On the jetty we met a patrol of young seamen in jungle green with long sleeves and long trousers as protection against mosquitoes, a tropical uniform we had never seen before. We had a chat with them, but they were not very communicative. Possibly they thought, from all our questions and surprise at such things as their uniform which they took for granted, that we must be a bit balmy. At any rate they gave us some rather odd looks.

After a while a boat came in with a midshipman in charge, and we went off in it to the ship. As we came alongside we saw the Commander at the top of the gangway having just changed for supper; and as I looked closer I was surprised to find it was Tom Masterman, a great friend of ours as he had been Staff Officer Operations to the C.-in-C., East Indies in 1941-42; we had been operating under him from June 1941 till we were sunk. He did not recognise us until we arrived on the quarter-deck; then was very surprised to see us and took us all along to the wardroom. Though we must have looked odd in our "uniform," thin faces and close cropped hair now growing again but not yet enough to make a parting, the others there were polite enough not to remark on our appearance.

Drinks were produced. We said, "Thanks, but please don't press us." And they did not. The warning was unnecessary as Tom had already given orders that P.O.W.s were to be allowed just one drink and if there were no ill effects perhaps the other half. We arranged to stay the night and cabins were put at our disposal. We had a wonderful supper, our first real European meal since we were captured.

After supper we were sent for by the Admiral, who welcomed us with great kindness and told us how pleased he was to see us. He was worried he said, about the safety of the P.O.W.s and internees, but had no men to spare to guard or take over even a portion of the town. He was surprised when I told him there were over four hundred sailors at Macassar; indeed it proved the first intimation he or anybody else in authority had received to the effect that there were naval P.O.W.s in the East Indies area. Although he and Captain Enright both stressed that they had come to help all nationalities and services, they left no doubt in our minds that charity begins at home. They very nearly sent me there and then in one of the two frigates, the *Loch Awe*, to Macassar with medical stores, but later decided to wait a day or two to see if the general position would clarify.

The Admiral said he would like to visit our camp at an early date and it was arranged for the day after tomorrow. We did not leave his cabin till late and then had a long chat with Masterman, before turning in and sleeping in a bunk with clean sheets.

Before breakfast next day we visited the slop room and got kitted out with some tropical whites, besides acquiring things like razors and other toilet articles. It felt quite strange to be back in correct uniform after years of "fancy dress," but when we got back to the camp we were laughed at. To the other P.O.W.s it was almost as if we had suddenly appeared in morning coats and toppers. After the indescribable sense of freedom we had experienced in being aboard a ship of the Royal Navy, going back behind bars was so frightful it depressed me for three days. Besides, for the first time I had heard of such things as radar, V-1s and Mulberry harbours, apart from a hundred other details of the war, and I felt very much out of everything. There was also the inner feeling that our compatriots who had come to rescue us, kind as they were to us, were probably saying, "They seem all right, but really they must be quite batty."

The Admiral turned up at the camp as promised. We put on a proper parade for him, formed a naval guard at the gate, and had one rating there to pipe him in. We wanted to hoist the White Ensign, but the flying of any national flags had been forbidden until the Nips had officially surrendered. I had had a White Ensign made during the period from August 15th especially for such an occasion, and it had been hidden away.

The Admiral had ordered that all the naval contingent were to be mustered in their barracks and not with the rest of the camp as he wished to have a friendly chat with the sailors first. I was in charge of this, and we had the White Ensign flying inside the barracks. The sailors were in great heart. The Admiral brought a shooting stick with him, and after I had reported the men to him, he sat on it and told everyone to cluster round. He just chatted with them. He told them that food was scarce and beer and tobacco expensive at home, but that everyone was in great spirit. He explained that he could not tell when we would go out, but assured us that this was right at the top of his priority list. As he left I called for three cheers and we nearly blew him out of the door. We gave him the White Ensign later and he flew it in H.M.S. *Sussex* on the day he shifted his flag at Singapore, making a general signal explaining his action. Later he gave it back to the Captain of *Jupiter*. This riled me rather because I felt I ought to have had it.

The other services were much impressed by Admiral Patterson. To begin with he was tactful - unlike a certain officer of R.A.P.W.I. (Repatriation of Allied Prisoners of War and Internees), the unit that had come in to get us out. I shall never forget the talk that particular officer gave us, telling us "to be patient" and that compared with what he had seen in Belsen and Buchenwald we were infinitely better off! Some people had just turned their backs on him and walked away. R.A.P.W.I. was quickly renamed Retain All Prisoners of War Indefinitely, a joke which they did not appreciate.

No one turned away from Admiral Patterson. He explained the situation precisely, he was amusing about it, and he left behind in the camp the conviction that he personally would do all he could to get us out.

Meanwhile Captain Enright was arranging to send help to the Macassar sailors. He suggested that I should fly there immediately, find the sailors if they had been moved into the hills, and come back and report what assistance they required; and he arranged a flight for me with the Dutch air authorities who had arrived to organise the air side of R.A.P.W.I.

I left on September 21st, taking the minimum of clothing in a pack and leaving the rest of my belongings in the Cycle Camp. The Nips did not know I was going, so it was like breaking out of school. I reported to a Dutch Air Force Officer but he knew nothing about me. Anyhow he said he would fit me in on a flight leaving that morning, but when I got to the aerodrome I found that our plane was bound for Singapore.

I told the man there, "I want to go to Balik Papan or Macassar but not Singapore."

"We are full up for Balik Papan and the plane for Macassar left at dawn," he said. "But if you go to Singapore you can take another plane back to Balik Papan."

"No," I said. "Once I get to Singapore I shall never get out of the place."

I went back to H.Q. at Batavia and had a row with the Dutchman. In the end he gave me a chit to say I could go in one of the Mitchells taking some Australians on repatriation through Balik Papan and Morotai. But it was up to one of the pilots to accept the extra weight. These planes were not due to leave till 1.30 p.m.

The pilots, when I found them, said it would be all right as there was plenty of wind and a long runway, only I would have to sit on the wireless set. Eventually I set off across the airfield to enter the aircraft, a very exciting moment. At last I was definitely flying out of Java, and there was to be no further hitch. We all piled in, some in the rear, some in the bomb bays, three or four of us behind the pilot's seat, and then we were off. I had not flown since 1929 and had only been up once before in my life.

We had a quick glimpse of Batavia behind us, then we were over the docks, with *Cumberland* at anchor, and soon after Java was gone. I have never seen it since. The time was 2 p.m. I remember being rather relieved at seeing the southern coast of Borneo come up, but passing over the jungles and great rivers it looked inhospitable and rather lonely.

At about 6 p.m. we suddenly saw the sea beyond, the Macassar Strait, and we were over Balik Papan. We went some way beyond it, then circled an airstrip which was obviously quite new - some tractors were still working on it.

Down we came, bumped rather hard, then bumped again and eventually came to rest in a cloud of dust. Waiting for us were about six jeeps manned by Australians. I got in marvelling at them but not prepared to admit I had never seen a jeep before, and away we went to a tented camp which accommodated a field ambulance unit of the 7th Australian Division.

What a welcome I got. After drinks - and there were doctors there to see I did not get too much - there was a marvellous supper, then a pow-wow late into the night. Hearing for the first time about things like penicillin, L.S.T.s, escort carriers and homing torpedoes, I felt like a Rip Van Winkle waking up to a new civilisation.

I slept that night on a comfortable camp bed in a tent which held about twenty sick. On each bed was a Red Cross parcel and a pair of pyjamas, a few novels, washing gear on a table close by, a reading light and some biscuits. It was heaven.

The 7th Australian Division had captured Morotai and then come on to Borneo early in July. A terrific naval bombardment lasting nearly a week had preceded the assault, so that the whole town had disappeared. Thousands of coconut trees stood at drunken angles, beheaded. The assault, made several miles to the north, had been pretty easy, but there had been some stiff fighting beyond the bridgehead. They had then built an airstrip and some piers, things beyond our imagination, and now they were clearing up the mess and collecting Japanese prisoners. One brigade had been sent over to Macassar to take the surrender. They were a fine crowd, this division of strapping, young, fit and cheerful, fighting Australians. They had fought a long battle from New Guinea and had never been defeated.

After breakfast next morning I took a jeep to the R.A.A.F. headquarters to see if I could get a flight over to Macassar. The driver of the jeep was a young farm lad from the outback, about nineteen, who said, "I am at your disposal, sir, and will take you wherever you want to go."

We set off bumping over dirt roads, my courteous driver handling the jeep with ease and quiet efficiency. I met several others like him in this division, each man a perfectly trained and integral part of a fighting machine that had been brought to a peak of perfection. On each one of them was the unmistakable stamp of victory.

As we approached a military camp some way ahead I said to my driver, "Is that Balik Papan?"

"No," he replied. "That was." And he pointed to a shell-blasted stretch of land where all that remained were a few tree stumps. I found a staff officer at the headquarters tent and asked for an aircraft to Macassar.

"That's easy," he said. "You can have a Mitchell tomorrow at ten. It will take you two or three hours to get there. And you can have one back the next day at noon. But I can't tell you how we can get you back to Batavia. Anyway come in again when you get back and we will see what we can do."

He was Jewish, full of drive and efficiency, and with a real Australian twang. He said he would make the arrangements and all I had to do was be on the airstrip at ten. Had I a jeep? Good. Well, best of luck. Glad to be of help.

We then drove on up a hill to the Australian general hospital, completely self-contained with comfortable wards, operating theatres, X-ray department and all the rest of it, all under canvas. There were more sick than wounded, but little or no malaria, which was a disciplinary offence for anyone in the division to have as it could be kept at bay with a daily dose of mepacrin.

I had actually come to see twelve sailors from Macassar who had been brought in with T.B., some in an advanced state. They were very surprised to see me and we exchanged P.O.W. news. I promised that I would see they got out as soon as they were fit.

I was also taken to see one of our boy ratings, a mental case. He never spoke and he did not recognise me, but I heard he recovered later.

The Australians insisted that I should call at their clothing store, and here I was issued with two suits of khaki tropical drill with long trousers, two pairs of pyjamas, socks, boots, two pullovers, besides other things. After years in rags it was a joy to go round a clothing store and pick what I liked.

As I was leaving the hospital I met a British naval officer and said, "Good afternoon."

"Hullo Cooper, where did you spring from?" he said to my surprise. "I haven't seen you for years."

"I'm sorry, but I don't remember who you are."

"You were a watch-keeper in the *Revenge* when I was doing my training in 1935, and I used to keep watch under you. My name is Marchington."

It transpired that he was Captain of an Australian frigate in the harbour - H.M.A.S. *Burdekan*. He said I must come and see his ship, and invited me to supper. I thanked him and said I would like to come about five, so that I could be shown round the ship and see all the new gadgets.

My driver took me back to the field ambulance for tea, and then brought me in again. I apologised that I would have to keep him waiting as I would not be coming back till late.

He said, "I am entirely at your disposal."

"Well then, come back at ten. I don't want to be too late as I am not very fit."

Marchington came for me in a boat and we went off to the ship. This was the first frigate I had seen, and was amazed at its equipment and fittings, most of them black magic to me. The C.O. of *Gascoigne*, the other frigate, came over and we had a great chat about the war.

My driver was waiting for me when I arrived back on shore, and we rattled back over the bumps in the dark. Next day, September 23rd, I left Balik Papan in a Mitchell for Macassar. I asked if we would land at Maros where, it will be recalled, our men had been sent to make an airstrip. The pilot said no, as that was now full of bomb holes, and advised me to hold on tight as the temporary strip they were using was very rough.

Coming in it looked very small to me, and it was rather frightening as the jungle came tearing towards us and I thought we were going into it, but we stopped just about twenty yards from the end of the strip.

When we had finally come to rest I dropped out of the hatch at the bottom, and who should I see standing there to meet me but E.R.A. Chandler, the stalwart who had led the Maros party for over two years. With him was another petty officer named Spicer and both were goggle-eyed with surprise. Of all the people they had expected to arrive in that aircraft, I was the least likely. At first they were not even quite certain it was me; I was properly dressed in tropical white uniform, and their memory of me did not go back beyond the ragged days.

"Well," I said. "I have come back. How's everyone?"

Then they went wild, and the other sailors there clustered round.

They led me to a table on the veranda of a hut, beckoned to some Nips and told them to bring lemon squash and bananas. Chandler was in charge of this strip; the Navy had made the Nips make it since the capitulation, and it was good to see the tables turned, our men ordering the Nips about instead of the other way around.

I stayed there about an hour and a half, until 1.45 p.m. when a South African rating arrived back with a high powered car and took me down to Macassar. We drove fast and I thoroughly enjoyed the sense of freedom, but coming into Macassar brought back all the painful memories of our first march as P.O.W.s, and of our departure, and of the lorry trips up to the cemetery to bury the dead.

The officers were living in a fine house on the coast road, which had once belonged to the camp dentist. The P.O.W. camp had been closed down and the ex-prisoners were accommodated in barracks just opposite this bungalow. It was called the Peace Camp. The White Ensign flew outside the officer's mess, which also served as a naval headquarters.

As we drove in, we passed a car coming out; inside it were the Padre and some warrant officers. They pulled up, all scarcely believing their eyes. We all got out and shook hands, but they had to leave as they were in a hurry to go to a conference with General Dougherty, the Australian fortress commander, and were late. The 21st Australian Infantry Brigade were in possession of the town.

They returned at 3.30 and we had a great reunion. The Padre was running the whole show, and had been doing the liaison with the Japanese, using French, through a naval staff officer. An hour later this Nip arrived up at the house and asked for the Padre personally.

The first thing he said was, "I hear your Senior Officer has returned."

"Yes," Gerald replied.

The officer then tried to find out why I had come back, and if there was any special reason, but the Padre made no definite reply. We were astonished how quickly the news of my arrival had reached the Nips. I had come a thousand miles and no one on the island could possibly have known I was coming. Yet after two years absence and a quick drive through the town, my presence had become known within an hour. Only in the East could news travel so fast.

Obviously the Nips were suspicious about my return, thinking that I was after them, and the Padre did nothing to put the man's mind at rest. Naturally I was out to get Yoshida whose tyranny had continued even after the capitulation; in fact he had been beating up people until three weeks before, when finally the Dutch adjutant had rung up the Nip H.Q. and said, "If you don't remove Yoshida from this camp I can't guarantee his safety."

It had reached a state when the prisoners might have suddenly taken care of him, and the adjutant did not want to risk an incident. The Nips had Yoshida out within an hour and since then he had disappeared. Rumour had it he was at Pare Pare, up the coast.

The men were far from well. They were all either very thin through malnutrition or puffy with beri-beri. Nearly all had beri-beri in some form or another and malaria. But they were very happy and morale was very high. They had never discovered where their officers had gone, and their first question was, "Have you seen the Captain?" To which I had to reply I knew nothing of him, except that he had gone to Japan.

That evening we had a great party, all the officers and the staff ratings together. A lot of sherry was drunk, and a cook produced some wonderful omelettes and coffee. At the end someone called for my health and I had to make a speech in reply. What they really wanted to know was when were they going out, and they hung on every word. They did not think I had come for nothing, so I explained why Admiral Patterson had sent me and told them I was flying back at noon next day to report to him in person. I said that from the start I had always predicted we would go out "grey funnel" and I still believed that. I added that from my experience in Java since capitulation no one knew from one day to the next when he was going.

"You are here one evening and gone the next morning, so not to worry. In the famous last words of the optimists, It won't be long now!"

That night I slept in a real bed - my first real bed since a night ashore in Colombo in October 1941. At 2 a.m. I was awakened by a noise in the hall below and went down to investigate and met the Padre doing the same. There were two British Army officers in the hall with some Australian officers, including the local Brigade Major, a man of about 6 ft. 6 in. I remember saying, "What the hell is happening in this house? Can't we get any sleep at all?"

The Brigade Major turned to me and said, "My dear fellow, all your chaps are going out in H.M.S. *Maidstone* at eight in the morning. You've got to get your people organised by then. That is what all the .... noise is about. Now get weaving." I got weaving, and when all had been organised, I went back to bed. I had already decided to go out with the men; I was not going back behind bars in Java if I could help it.

Next morning we rose early, and after breakfast I went over to the Peace Camp to meet the men. I had arranged for them to parade at 7 a.m. to ensure there were none adrift in the town. It was good seeing their faces again, all grinning, and I told them what was going to happen. It was our final release, and a very emotional moment. I cannot remember what I said, but it seemed to go down well enough. We then mustered on the road to prepare for our move to the docks.

The idea was for the whole draft to be moved in some lorries doing a shuttle service. At the docks, we would embark in two Australian minesweepers, the *Inverelle* and the *Barcoo*, which were to take us out to the entrance to the channel where *Maidstone* was anchored.

The men were a bit out of hand, and excited. No one seemed to be taking charge. I was sitting in the Brigade Major's car on the opposite side of the road waiting for the first lorry loads to drive off, when suddenly a fight started.

Our men had given a wireless set to an Indonesian and some Dutchmen had tried to take it off him in the road. The British had gone to his assistance and a fight spread quickly between the two European nationals. There was a big crowd of Indonesians in the roadway, and they started to move forward to join in the fray. The Brigade Major was shouting at the top of his voice in an attempt to restore order, but no one took the slightest notice. I jumped out of the car and shot across the road. By calling out the names of the men in the thick of the fight, and by telling them to obey me or I would leave them behind, I managed to make them break off.

Meanwhile the Indonesians had regained the wireless set, the bone of contention, and peace was soon restored. I went over to the men and quietly told them that they would have to comply with any orders I gave them, or stay behind. I dread to think what might have happened if the fight had got out of hand as the natives were quite hostile. It was a good thing I was on the spot as sailors do not like being ordered about by soldiers.

The Brigade Major then took me to his headquarters. He went in first to see General Dougherty and told him about the fight. Then I was called in, and found myself face to face with a man under forty

Prisoners-of-War from Macassar landing from H.M.S. Maidstone at Fremantle, Western Australia

with a D.S.O. and bar on his chest. I told him about my journey from Java, that these were my men, that I knew them well and could handle them, but I was due to return to Batavia at noon. I looked appealingly at him.

"You seem to be the only one who can control them at the moment," he said.

"Yes, I think I am," I replied.

"What you are asking me to do is to command you to go out with them in *Maidstone*, isn't it? Well I do command you. When you get on board, make a signal - your wireless is better than mine - to the authorities at Batavia and say you were ordered to go in *Maidstone* by the Fortress Commander."

I was delighted and relieved.

"You are going to Fremantle in Western Australia. The Lord Mayor of Perth is a great friend of mine. I will write you a letter of introduction." Busy though he was, he had the goodness to do this personal act of kindness for me.

At the docks, I found all the men embarked in the two minesweepers. There were over four hundred of them and the decks were cluttered. The Captain of the *Maidstone* was on the jetty, and also the Dutch adjutant who had come to see us off. A few minutes before we sailed General Dougherty arrived. He went along the jetty shaking hands with the sailors he could reach. They were all shouting to him - "Mind you get Yosh", "Good old Twenty-first", "Thanks for coming to fetch us".

As the wires were slipped I stood on the edge of the bridge and called for three cheers for the General and the 21st Australian Infantry Brigade, and the noise was terrific. As we moved slowly away from the jetty he stood at the salute, smiling. By then nearly every sailor was shouting. "Mind you get Yosh", "Don't let Yosh get away", "Don't forget Goldie".

The General just flicked his right little finger in the air. It was a gesture which said, "Never fear, I'll get him." And he kept his word.

It took us an hour's steaming to reach *Maidstone*. We went alongside her port side abreast the fore waist and a gangway was put over. The Captain went up first and I went next, to be received by a red-bearded Commander. The rest followed. At last we could say we were free, on board a ship flying the White Ensign. We were going home "grey funnel."

We sailed at 2 p.m. for Fremantle. The rest of the day was a kind of daze. After years that seemed endless, years of privation, of humiliation, and indignities to our race and uniform, without hope of retaliation, it was now all over. The spectre of death from hunger and disease had vanished.

The enemy had sought to break our spirit by malice, but in fact had only made us prouder of our country and service than ever before; which proved the old saying of Admiral Blake that the English should only be punished by the English, as they could never be cowed by foreigners.

Many of our comrades had died, but undoubtedly there would have been many more but for the adaptability, the cheerfulness and the indefatigable spirit of the British seaman in adversity.

But there was more to it than that. As Padre FitzGerald so aptly quoted from the 124th Psalm, *Nisi quia Dominus* - "If the Lord Himself had not been on our side...."

The author in command of the destroyer Onslaught on return to naval service in 1946

Postscript

The date the Japanese had forecast for the invasion of Nippon was November 1st, 1945. It was the deadline too for the massacre of all prisoners-of-war and internees in their hands. Thus would they show the world that no holds were barred in the last desperate struggle for their homeland.

The dropping of the atomic bombs on Hiroshima and Nagasaki averted that struggle. The bombs unfortunately caused the death of thousands of innocent civilians, but they saved many more lives that inevitably must have been lost in a protracted war. And they saved us.

As for our guards, justice followed close on their heels. Yoshida was in due course arrested, and with his fellow tyrants brought to trial before a War Crimes tribunal. I wrote an affidavit for the tribunal, but it was only a fraction of the indictment. They were condemned to death by hanging.

Some years after the war a high-ranking Dutch naval officer told me that, on hearing his sentence, Yoshida had asked if he could meet his end by shooting, rather than by hanging, because he was a fighting man. This had been granted, and Yosh, as he faced the firing squad, had shouted *Banzai* for his Emperor just as the shots rang out. His prophesy that he would leave his bones in the East Indies had been fulfilled.

Appendix

A document, now in the Imperial War Museum, had been issued to every P.O.W. camp before the end of the War ordering every prisoner to be killed when the assault on Japan started. This read as follows:

> "Whether they are destroyed individually or in groups, or however it is done, with mass bombing, poisonous smoke, poisons, drowning, decapitation or what, dispose of them as the situation dictates. In any case, it is the aim not to allow the escape of a single one, to annihilate them all, and not leave any trace."

This document was used after the War at the trial of General Tojo, who was condemned to death by hanging.